DEAR CHILDREN

DEAR CHILDREN

Christiane Collange

Translated by Gillian Willy

ARROW BOOKS

Arrow Books Limited
62–65 Chandos Place, London WC2N 4NW

An imprint of Century Hutchinson Limited

London   Melbourne   Sydney   Auckland
Johannesburg and agencies throughout
the world

First published in France as *Chers Enfants* by Fayard 1987
First published in Great Britain 1989

© Librairie Arthème Fayard 1987
Translation © Gillian M. Willy 1989

Photoset by Deltatype Ltd, Ellesmere Port
Printed and bound in Great Britain by
Anchor Press Ltd, Tiptree, Essex

ISBN 0 09 960680 1

ACKNOWLEDGMENTS

Thanks first of all to my four dear children. Once again, if they hadn't existed, this book certainly wouldn't have been written – not by me anyway!

Then I should like to thank all those who took as great an interest in this subject as I did myself, and who helped me enrich the book with information, not only impressions: Catherine Gros supervised all the research; Renée Raymond prepared the press files; Puck Simonnet, President of the 'Club L', helped me with my questionnaire to the members; Françoise Frisch, President of 'Synesis', organized a group meeting on fathers' attitudes; Michel-Louis Levy of the Institut National d'Etudes Demographiques, encouraged and supervised my venture into demography.

Finally, my thanks to everyone, men and women, who talked to me about their children, those that they had . . . and the others.

CONTENTS

Why? Children expressed in decimal points. Countries full of little old people. How unfair! The German flame is burning lower and lower. Specifically German reasons. East German policy.

The horror of a back-street abortion. When sex and procreation went hand-in-hand. The revolution in contraception. For the future: contragestion. Being active not passive. The child-wish won't go away. The imaginary last child. Mini-poll of career women. Mini-poll of women at home.

Different categories of fathers. In search of experienced fathers. About the child-wish. About pregnancy and birth. About everyday life. About upbringing. Fathers are nostalgic for the old days. Mini-poll of men.

Approaching forty. Those responsible for the 'baby flop'. A surge of fashion for parenthood. A return to wedding rings. Eight unusual ways of becoming parents. 1. Acknowledgment of natural children. 2. The about-turn by childless women approaching forty. 3. 'Afterthoughts' stage a come-back. 4. Children of second marriages are on the increase. 5. Triumphant polygamists. 6. Deliberate single parents. 7. Sterility's multiple pregnancies. 8. Adoptions by couples who want a child to love. Bifurcation: birthrate-depopulation. The generation of caring women.

Sole depository for all their ambitions. Only child or first child with no successor. We really should talk about death. The Catherine generation. The Collange conviction. Divorce isn't so hard on several children. The 'big jobs' joke. Catherine and John: afraid of a second child. For the parents' enjoyment as well.

Introduction

Don't say child, say children

Yes, it really is me, the author of *I'm your Mother*, who is trying to convince men and women of today not to say child, but children. Don't say baby, say babieS with an 'S'.

Not a cowering, defeated little 's' like those written at the end of vast families in days gone by, but a huge, readable, positive, deliberate 'S', nicely rounded like a pregnant woman. The 'S' which is worrying demographers, preoccupying politicians and threatening the pensioners of the year 2015 by its absence. The 'S' which young mothers dream about more often than you think, even though they don't always fulfil their desire for babies.

This 'S' doesn't necessarily mean six, eight or ten children. In the West, maxi-families belong to the 19th century; it's only in developing countries that they still exist at the end of the 20th century. But it certainly does mean two children, preferably three – why not four?

It's surprising, I know. Having been in the vanguard of the mothers' revolt against these 'little things' when they were growing up, and having received thousands of letters from parents, particularly mothers, from all over the world approving my criticism of post-adolescents, how dare I sit down at my keyboard now to advise other adults of the next generation not only to become parents *without fail*, but also to have at least one child, preferably two or more.

I can't see any contradiction between these two attitudes. You can swear at someone for letting you down or irritating you even though you're perfectly well aware that their absence and your loneliness would be just as hard to bear as the annoyance of a conflicting relationship, which is only temporarily unsatisfactory after all.

When has reading novels about unhappy love affairs ever dissuaded anyone from falling in love? Even if all love affairs don't lead to diamond weddings, does that mean they shouldn't be experienced? Life is made to be rich, varied, full to overflowing with people, happenings and things which prove by their presence and the complications they provoke that you are alive and able either to face up to them or take pleasure in them. By too readily trying to avoid difficulties, arguments, people who irritate you, dangers, troublemakers and disappointments, you risk falling into the rhythms of a dehumanized daily routine.

The heart needs exercise

You can put up with yourself better if you have to learn to put up with others first. Bachelorhood and childlessness lead to depression and paranoia more often than an excess of partners or children. As a television publicity campaign put it: 'Get your heart moving'. In this case they're talking about the physical heart – they're advising us to make it beat more quickly, more often, to keep the pump in good working order for as long as possible. The emotional heart also needs exercise to make sure it's functioning well and staying active all your life. Children give it violent and regular exercise and can be relied on to keep it warm.

Children are tiring – they take away your freedom, cost a lot, shake you out of your routine, take up an enormous amount of their parents' time, and aren't always as grateful as they should be. Even so, I don't know a better way of finding a purpose in life, a reason for being born and an excuse for dying. They are the best remedy for loneliness – a drastic remedy sometimes because our kids have a perpetual need for the home base that Mum and Dad represent even if they don't live together any longer. It's the only permanent refuge from the rough and tumble of the modern world.

In the course of present day existence, you change more and more often – home, job, life style, friends, colleagues or even partners; only one relationship remains the same all your life: the one between parents and children. Through stormy rows and reconciliations, tenderness and irritation, you keep from beginning to end the same parents, the same children, the same ties and shared memories of twenty years or more.

After the vicissitudes of life an individual, on approaching old age, often goes back to his beginnings. Just listen to the really old who never tire of telling stories about their childhood. The familiar expression 'in their second childhood' couldn't be more apt! Thanks to progress in gerontology, the threat of physical decrepitude has become more and more distant, and the over-eighties take refuge in their earliest memories to an amazing extent. It's as though the 'biological' family is the one certainty to hang on to before finally letting go.

That doesn't mean that these 'biological' family relationships are simpler because they are more 'natural'; quite the opposite is the case, as all the psychiatrists agree. The unbreakable tie is a double-edged sword which aggravates, clashes, grudges and guilt at the same time as it encourages patience, forbearance and leniency so that, on the whole, the relationship can be summed up as positive.

In the old days, when marriage was for life, the matrimonial tie was as long-lasting as the filial tie, and one would take the place of the other. We have all been told stories by our grandfathers and great-grandfathers of irretrievable breakdowns between parents and children brought on by differences of opinion over religion, social background, interests or character. Today, these quarrels until death hardly ever arise. Are we more tolerant these days than our forbears? Yes, we certainly are, but we're more sensible too.

The only 'life and death' tie

The marriage relationship, weakened as it is these days by co-habitation, break-ups and divorce, represents less of an emotional security than original family ties. How many young people are prepared to cut off their parental relationship from their life as a couple? If everyone gets on well, all the better. If there are clashes or rejections on one side or the other, or both, one keeps one's distance without breaking off completely. On Sundays and for a few days during the summer holidays or over Christmas and New Year, each one comes back to spend a bit of time 'at home' without the other taking umbrage. Emotionally speaking, no-one is going to put all their eggs into one vulnerable new basket – your own family seems a lot less likely to pack up! And when things go wrong, someone can always be found to lend a sympathetic ear and soothe conjugal wounds.

Parents are sensible too. Secret hopes of a possible/ probable break-up make one much more tolerant. There- fore we put up with these disappointing partners – our children are always incomparably better in our eyes than their chosen companions – because we alone wield the ultimate weapon of the 'life and death' tie.

It's also a double-edged weapon because the children take advantage of it to lean on us as heavily as they possibly can all our/their lives. An experienced mother said to me once:

'When you are young parents you believe that your lives will sort themselves out better when the children are bigger, and this gives you courage and hope to help you face up to the thousands of daily problems when they're tiny. The bigger they get, the more you realise how wrong you were. When the children are big, they disrupt their parents' world even more radically – particularly the mothers' – because there is no longer a general management to run the family enterprise, but two separate organizations whose interests sometimes coincide but are sometimes wide apart, and which constantly have to take into account the needs, timetables and financial potential of everyone. Thank goodness memories of babyhood make you forget the horrors of that period!'

A somewhat pessimistic view of parents' lot. After all, you don't only exist on hopes and memories. There is also the immediate present with its thousands of small delights, smiles, looks, hugs, steps forward – all magic moments to be enjoyed together. This side of things is hardly even discussed these days.

Children don't rate very highly in the papers unless they represent a medical victory over sterility. Frozen embryos make page one, but most national newspaper editors prefer to talk about losing weight than having babies.

The prevailing atmosphere, worries about unemployment, economic difficulties, stagnation of purchasing power, insecurity, working women, new relationships between men and women and the dizzying increase in divorce hardly militate in favour of a triumphant birthrate. Even so, I am convinced that children, if regarded as stocks and shares, are still a good investment in the enterprise of life.

They have a value which we must rediscover now, at the end of this century, having shaken the dust off them, brought them up to date, and readapted them to suit ourselves. We're not at all the same parents that our parents were. Our children won't be the same parents as we were for them. In this area too, motivations and relationships need to be re-thought. Now that the place of the couple, the place of work and the place of sex in our daily lives have all been reconsidered, one can feel a shockwave hitting the family. Whenever a great upheaval is proclaimed, the end of an era, a complete transformation in human behaviour – every time it has to do with couples, work or sex – this re-thinking results in progress, adaptation, the throwing off of taboos, but never in total rejection of the previous order.

Except, sometimes, in the case of those children who haven't always had time to be born by the time their potential parents realize how much better it would be if they had existed. . . .

I think that's a pity, and I feel I really must say so.

Marvellous memories of lots of us

Why this urge to take sides? Where do I get this need to line myself up with the birthrate enthusiasts? Obviously from my own personal experience.

I've never complained about belonging to a large family, very much the opposite. There were five of us at home, and I have marvellous memories of lots of us.

Daddy, who was a journalist, travelled a lot, and liked to take Mummy with him to see the world. So my maternal grandmother often looked after our gang of temporary orphans. Honestly, we were none the worse for it. What difference did it make whether we sat down six or eight to table? We certainly missed our parents less than some of our friends who were only children – they were left all alone when their parents went out to dinner or the cinema, reducing the household by two-thirds.

I always felt that the jealousies, injustices, antagonisms and conflicts inherent in all families – parents/children, children/children, parents amongst themselves, etc – were settled much more easily because we were so numerous. If one annoyed me, another made me laugh. If some made me cry, others comforted me, so our parents didn't need to get involved in all our little upsets.

Mummy and Daddy each had their favourites. Differing in temperament, age and sex, we complemented one another, and could take over from our parents and help them to provide support during the difficult and critical periods which all of us went through from time to time.

I need hardly say that, having arrived in fourth place as third daughter to a mother who really only liked boys and had been longing for a second son ever since his older brother was born, I was greatly 'liberated' by the birth of a little boy in fifth place, although I didn't quite realize it at the time. At last, seven years after the awful disappointment caused by my arrival, my mother had another son, who made up for my birth once and for all!

Today my little brother is actually very big – extremely satisfied, it seems to me, with his position as an 'afterthought' – although, logically, his birth should never have been registered at all.

My mother's 'afterthought'

My mother often told us the story of her 'afterthought'. She suddenly realized she was pregnant and decided then and there not to go through with it.

It was 1937. Hitler was terrifying the more clear-minded Europeans by his threats of war and his anti-Jewish proclamations. With four children already to be protected in time of war and a husband of Jewish origin, there was no logical argument to justify this fifth child. In addition, Mummy was over thirty-five and at that time, before the days of scanners and reliable tests, childbirth late in life had a bad reputation. Mummy went to see my father who was in Bordeaux on business, to let him know she had quite decided not to keep the baby. It was better to face up to the horror and danger of a back-street abortionist than to expose a little child to the dangers of a second world war and extermination by the Nazis.

My mother hadn't taken into account the irrational life force which sometimes pushes men and women into wanting children for no other reason than their desire for them.

Daddy belonged to that race of fathers described by Peguy as 'modern day romantics'. He knew how to shoot Love's arrow deep into women's hearts. When she got into the train that would take her back to Paris to 'do what had to be done', Mummy found a little bunch of violets and a card on her reserved seat. The card said 'Please keep this one for me!' How could anyone resist such a request?

So that's how my little brother came to be born, just before the war. Until 1944, this decision didn't seem very sensible. Since then, everyone has congratulated themselves on it.

Please don't think I'm running an anti-abortion campaign; at times I've been embroiled in the opposite camp. With regard to contraception and abortion, I have always stood up for the right of women to use their bodies as they choose, to make either love or children. A child shouldn't be born because of an irreparable mistake or moral or social pressure. Even if the baby isn't planned down to the last day, the idea that he is going to exist in the near future must awaken in his parents positive feelings of hope, curiosity, enthusiasm and pleasure, which are far stronger than any number of sensible, well thought out negative decisions.

Children by chance and children by choice

Having had four children myself, two more or less by chance and two by choice – in-between time, in common with millions of other women, contraceptives having become a part of my daily routine – I have never regretted my children who came either by chance or by choice.

Incidentally, they haven't complained about my chances and choices either. In fact, they rather liked the overcrowded, boisterous and somewhat chaotic state of the houses we shared while they were growing up.

Out of the four, the one who really wasn't part of the planned programme was the second. His arrival was totally unexpected. Certain pregnancies don't start strictly according to the timetable, but they are in the air to the extent that they are a welcome surprise. That wasn't the case at all when, at twenty-two years old, I realized I was expecting another child. My older son was about three months old. You can imagine the sort of questions his father and I asked ourselves! Nevertheless, deep down, I couldn't find any powerful enough negative impulses to give me the courage to face up to an abortion. Somewhat by fatalism, a lot by fear of damaging my health, but also because of my trust in life, I 'kept' this second baby.

A thousand times since, when I see him laughing, struggling, succeeding, loving, thinking, building a life for himself, taking his own little boy into his arms, I've remembered how anxious I felt at being a mother again at such a young age. He so nearly didn't exist! And that would have been a great shame for me, and even more so for his brother who, thanks to him, had the sort of wonderful childhood that only a couple of little boys as close as they were could experience. They were as inseparable as twins, but without the excessive dependence on one another that sometimes exists between identical pairs. Without doubt his would have been the greater loss if his brother had never been born!

It's rare that children resent their parents for having given them life. At times of worries and difficulties, adolescent crises or unhappy love affairs, they sometimes question their existence, but the vast majority admit that they are quite satisfied with the chance or choice that gave them a part to play in the Great Comedy.

If you had your life all over again . . .

'If you had your life all over again?' I was often asked this question by journalists or readers when my last book came out.[1] I was the mother who criticized her children's attitudes, was irritated by their casualness, disappointed by their monumental selfishness and was all for severing the umbilical cord – but if I had my life all over again, I'd do exactly the same without any hesitation or doubt whatever. The overall assessment is positive – even super-positive.

For more than thirty years my four dear children have filled my heart and mind with so many feelings and happenings, ordinary everyday details and fundamental

1. *Moi, ta Mère* Ed. Fayard 1985; pocket book edition 1986. *I'm Your Mother* Arrow Books 1987.

decisions, that I haven't had time to notice how my life was racing by. I've never had the spare time to brood about the absurdity of the human condition or the hopelessness of a destiny which is bound to end in death.

Like all parents of several children, I've always been astonished by the great reserves of enthusiasm, anxiety, determination and weakness which have four times enabled me to marvel, exert myself, hope, be disappointed and hope once more! No, the first smiles, the first awakenings, the first steps, the first words, the first reasonings, the first challenges of a child – of one alone – haven't satisfied my compulsive appetite for discovery. Each time I've been knocked sideways by the vital force which drives these little things into understanding and carrying out such complicated processes. Four completely home-made experiences haven't made me blasé. I still have reserves of wonder which allow me to appreciate my grandchildren's first efforts at speech without getting bored.

Each child is unique, unpredictable and different from the others. Right from the first weeks you can watch the tiny baby's individual temperament beginning to form and guess what he will be like during his childhood, even all his life. Parents can make more of this initial capital, or dissipate it, but they can't transform it completely. It's always amazing to see such different personalities emerging from the same kind of upbringing, the same group of people, sharing the same way of life and thinking. This variety partly explains the pleasure I got from having several children. I'm incorrigible – my only tiny regret is not to have had one, or even two more. . . .

The Herculean task of working mothers

No doubt I would have had a more dazzling career if I hadn't given up so much time to my little gang. Perhaps my breasts would have been a little less heavy and my figure more girlish. I would certainly have travelled more or saved more money. I would obviously have been more cultured. What else?

I would have worn myself out less, and would have worried and lost my temper less. But I would also have laughed less, loved less and lived less. Above all, I would have missed all those warm babies' bodies, all those trusting, childish looks, all those first smiles/steps/words/ arguments – all those inconsolable little moments of unhappiness which only I could put right, all those bumps which I kissed better, all those achievements when I was rewarded with a look of pride, all those shared secrets, all those setbacks which I took on myself – all those joys whether gratuitous or deliberate.

If I had my life to live all over again, I'd do exactly the same . . . that's an absurd statement. You can't interpret your role in two ways by altering the script! In the case of women in particular, a day comes long before old age, when the machine is no longer in working order. This moment of maturity is easier to live with if you are satisfied with your previous choices.

And then, it's not the first time I've spoken up in favour of mothers at home. A few years ago I published *Je veux rentrer a la maison*[2] (*I Want to Go Home*). What an outcry that caused in the feminist camp at the time! I'd wanted to describe the Herculean task of being a working mother. Here's an example of the sort of thing they almost invariably say to each other when they leave their offices or shops:

'What are you going to do now?'

'I want to go home. The children are expecting me, and I've got shopping to do and the dinner to get ready – my daughter wants me to go over her French composition with her . . .'

I wanted help for us, I wanted someone to hurry up and rearrange our working hours, allow us to stop work for a few years when our children were small without prejudicing our professional lives for ever. I felt that our careers shouldn't be planned in exactly the same way as men's were, and that the fact that we bear the children and carry

2. Ed. Grasset 1979; pocket book edition 1980.

out practically all the household tasks should be taken into consideration.

In other words, I was speaking up for women like myself who wanted to have children but were not prepared to give up everything else in life because of them.

I was called a renegade, traitress, reactionary, even a fossil. I just had to forget it because I'm not the sort to bear a grudge. How did I dare renounce the struggle for Women's Liberation in such a mundane way by reminding everyone that it's not easy to reconcile one's professional and domestic lives?

A rather primitive urge

Ideas have evolved considerably during seven years of feminist reflection; mine haven't. Today voices are heard demanding more consideration and respect for the primordial aspect of the feminine condition known as the Maternal Function. Betty Friedan and Germaine Greer of the USA and Australia, and Anne-Marie de Vilaine and a group of thirty researchers and women writers in France, have clearly watered down their feminism.

As for myself, I can repeat almost word for word what I wrote at the time as an introduction:

'I refuse to choose between my future as a career woman and my life as a mother.

I refuse to die of boredom, or overwork . . .

I don't believe in either the crusade for liberation or unconditional sacrifice by women.

I don't consider myself either a factory machine or a domestic appliance.

I want to live.

I want everything at the same time.'

Since I wrote those lines I've met thousands of European

mothers. They nearly all express themselves the same way. Sadly, many of them despair of achieving their aim, particularly the young ones. Unable to change their professional status soon enough, they decide to restrict their families. How often have I heard them say rather wistfully that they would have loved another child, but it just wasn't possible?

What a pity to have got to that stage! Young couples have been forced into a position of being careful and civilized, in debt and unsettled, with the result that more and more often they resist the rather crazy and somewhat primitive urge to have children.

It is said that a lower birthrate is the indisputable mark of the most advanced societies. This 'progress' worries me. From the age of twenty onwards it transforms the young into people who have retired early – they're a little apprehensive and sad at the thought of their future which they know in advance they won't dare to fill with as many children as they would like.

This book is aimed primarily at young people, to describe the joys and riches of this 'S' – to try and convince them to have more babies.

Next, it's aimed at everyone else, to ask them to strive together to transform the general atmosphere, to change people's habits and to re-establish the rules of our society so that, in future, the chances of being born remain the same, or even greater, than the risks of dying.

I

When Children Disappear

To have or not to have another child? That is the question.

Frankly, it isn't all that much easier to solve than Hamlet's. It's just as essential. Merely asking it is already providing a bit of a counterweight to the bad reputation children have in our somewhat individualistic society.

The present generation of young adults, both boys and girls, have less and less contact with babies and young children. It's increasingly rare for them to have little brothers and sisters – any they do have tend to be much the same age as themselves.

These days, thanks to contraception, medical abortion and progress in obstetrics and perinatal care, big sisters no longer have to bring up babies for their mothers who have been worn out by countless pregnancies and miscarriages. Since the days are gone when generations of young men are decimated by war, and thanks to longer life expectancy for men,[1] big brothers no longer need to take their father's place when their mother has been left a widow with tiny children. Therefore many reach the age of adulthood, or prolonged post-adolescence, without ever having held a baby in their arms or shared everyday life with anyone less than ten years old. Not even a nephew or niece, or even the baby belonging to a couple of friends because most couples of their generation, whether married or living together, postpone 'ordering' their first child till later on.

1. In a century and a half men's life expectancy has increased from 39 to 71.2.

The young don't handle babies any more

Daniel, young father of a few months-old baby, admits:

'Apart from my son, I'd never handled a baby in my life, and neither had my wife. With the result that when Jeremy was born we were both equally scared we might break him! Boys doing their military service should be made to spend a few days in a nursery, and so should girls, when they apply to take their driving test. At school you do pottery and football, but nobody teaches you this astonishing thing – physical contact with a tiny little body!'

There's only one exception: when parents remarry after a divorce. The children of the first marriage then have the opportunity of getting to know children smaller than themselves through the introduction of a half-brother or sister. I've noticed that as long as these 'halves' don't arrive too soon, and plenty of affectionate advance warning is given, they are generally greeted with enthusiasm by the older children, who appreciate this widening of the family circle more than they fear it.

In this way my older sons had three brothers and a sister in the space of four years: two from their father and two from me. This environment filled with small children in no way discouraged their own paternal 'vocations'. The older one, way ahead of his generation, already had two sons by the time he was twenty-eight. Just between us I think – and I very much hope – that he and his wife won't stop there!

Big towns without the patter of tiny feet

Children really like other children, and it's only as they grow up that they gradually lose this natural inclination. Because they are out of touch with the specific charm of small people, young couples aren't aware – and even dread to admit – that babies are one of the pleasures of life.

In certain large Western towns in Germany and New York, for instance, yuppies or dinkys (double income no kids yet) no longer see any prams or men and women with babies in their arms. Most parents with young children move out to the suburbs to avoid the huge rates in city centres. I've often wondered whether part of the charm of Paris or Madrid lies in the fact that it's still possible to find yourself walking beside a pram when on a pedestrian crossing, or to watch children coming out of nursery or primary schools. I just can't resist these little things when they come running out of school all grubby, carrying satchels on their backs which are always too big for their diminutive frames. Part of the attraction of the parks and gardens of these big cities is that every day of the year tiny children make their first tentative steps near the sandpits. Every Christmas afternoon brand-new roller skates and bicycles, brought by Father Christmas the night before, are tried out here for the first time.

As children get scarcer old people, because of living longer, are multiplying, with the result that the urban landscape has got wrinkled with age and has changed from a children's holiday camp to an old people's home.

While travelling in Egypt in 1985 I was very impressed by the sight of Cairo's streets. Its galloping birthrate is terrifying, and is a danger to the country's economic balance. Every nine months, the Egyptian population increases by a million inhabitants.[2] It's a country bursting at the seams with babies, children and young people. In contrast with India or Black Africa where the children look haggard and underfed, Egyptian children are smiling and seem fairly content. My travelling companions appeared rather horrified by the excessive hordes of urchins, sometimes hanging on in threes and fours to their mother's djellabah, who looked young enough to be their sister. Tourists in search of the remains of the Pharoahs can see for themselves the extent of the population explosion which

2. The Egyptian population was 48.3 million in mid-1985 with the birthrate figure of 5.3 children per woman. Birthrate figures of over 5 are mainly found in Africa and Moslem countries. India, for example, has a present birthrate figure of 4.5.

has been taking place for the last twenty years along the African shores of the Mediterranean.

Fear is a bad argument

Comparing public gardens in Nice with the streets of Algiers or Cairo obviously provides food for thought! However I don't wish to resort to this sort of argument in order to urge people to stop the downward curve of the birthrate. Economists, planners, demographers and politicians have been using it for the last fifteen years and don't seem to have convinced anyone to have children *by fear*.

Racist fear of our country being invaded by immigrants from overpopulated countries with inadequate resources; fear of the disappearance of the white race; materialist fear of non-payment of pensions; fear of the year 2000; fear of the decline of Western civilisation – fear is never an incentive to reproduce. On the contrary, by talking of the future in terms of the apocalypse, people have been given the best possible excuse for not having children: why bring children into the world if economic crisis and unemployment appear to be unavoidable, if the rich countries are to be swamped by hordes from the overcrowded Third World and if, in the 21st century, the population of the world is to be condemned to instantaneous extermination by a bomb, or slower death by atomic contamination?

You can't persuade young couples to have children by collective arguments – in the name of more allowances for workers, of the Country, of Westerners or even of God! Hitler certainly succeeded by it, but don't blame me for disagreeing with that particular person's methods!

Herve Le Bras, a representative of new demography, looks at the way people live rather than just counting heads, and he says:

'With regard to a policy for increasing the birthrate, I think it is a mistake to put the question in national rather than family terms. The cry is always "Children for the nation" which is no longer heeded, whereas it would be much better to say "Support for the Family". We haven't made enough effort to draw our conclusions from the "privatisation" of the birthrate. To be perfectly frank, the discussion on the birthrate is actually discouraging people not only from having a third child, but from having one in the first place!'

We always consider people very intelligent when they clearly express our own views. I found this observation of Herve Le Bras quite remarkable.

Children are the end-product of a series of altogether personal decisions, of vital impulses, of the search for individual fulfilment and of a sort of long-term emotional security. Each child is justified much more in terms of his parents' individual present and future than from a national, collective or worldwide perspective. I've always thought, for example, that candidates for parenthood never envisage their baby as a bad-tempered, idle, spotty adolescent, even less as a pop fan who they will be rubbing noses with every day in fifteen or twenty years' time. If so, the birthrate would have gone down to nought since the introduction of contraception. All the reasons for having children have been challenged in modern society. A brief comparative table shows how traditional motives have become outdated in our Western civilization (most traditional motives still remaining valid in developing countries).

COMPARATIVE TABLE

In the old days you had children . . .	Today . . .
Because you couldn't do anything else.	Contraception means birth control.

Because all religions (especially the Catholics) told you to.

Religious practice is greatly diminished. Even practising Catholics don't always respect the dogma of 'the rhythm method'.

Because you were afraid of dying from an abortion due to the bad state of prophylactics.

Abortion on demand, as its name implies, means not having to risk either your life or your future fertility.

In order to do the same as everyone else.

The one- or two-child family has become the norm.

To prove you could do it. Having lots of children was a continual proof of fertility.

Still a valid argument for a first child but it doesn't stand up after that. Fertility no longer has any great social merit, upward mobility being on the whole easier for small families.

For passing on your name. Successions of girls only result from frantic quests for boys to carry on the family name.

Apart from royal families, those of 'blue blood' or Rothschilds, the cult of the family name is rapidly vanishing which is proof of the disappearance of the patriarchy.

To hand on your land, your worldly goods, your workshop or your pair of leather boots.

From now on, inheritances will only be of benefit, and then probably only moderately, towards the end of your life. Parents set up their children during their lifetime, and are often retired grandparents before inheriting from their own parents.

To pass on knowledge or a skill.

The technological revolution has rendered parents' knowledge obsolete. They have enough difficulty keeping 'with it' without having to see to the development of the young, who are taken care of by society (not always all that well!).

To improve your standard of living by exploiting them and sending them out to work too early.

Young people start working life later and later. When they do start earning their living it doesn't often occur to them to make sure their parents profit from it!

For security in old age. The more children you had, and the more you ensured they had a 'good situation' by paying for their education or helping to set them up, the less risk you had of ending up impoverished towards the end of your life.

Old age is setting in later and later, and you don't think about it at all when you have your children – except in a few cases of belated pregnancies. So we're talking about emotional rather than material security. State assistance, retirement and old age pensions etc count more than children when it comes to guaranteed living standards for retired wage earners.

To sum up, all the arguments need to be rethought. Discussions on family and emotional culture, and their portrayal, need to be brought radically up to date if there is to be any chance of arresting the decline in birthrate.

It's by making love

First of all, an important rediscovery: it's more 'normal' to have children than not to do so. In the whole of nature, life flows from birth to death via reproduction. Whether you believe in God or not doesn't really matter – you still marvel at the subtle, ingenious and effective ways by which different reproductive systems enable existing living beings to perpetuate themselves. In particular we must take our hats off to that of the mammals, our own particular group, for having been programmed down to the last chromosome.

The birth of every test tube baby is a source of wonder, but much more fantastic is the fact that thousands and thousands of foetuses are formed by a technology which is as complex as it is easy and pleasant to set in motion . . . as long as one remembers the connection which still exists between sex and procreation! Having disassociated the two notions, I often wonder whether the under-twenty-fives still know that babies are conceived by making love! When we talk to them about these things it's always to explain the drawbacks and to warn them against diseases which are transmitted in the same way as ovaries are fertilized. It's hardly ever to extol the joys of physical love coupled with the ulterior motive of having a child together.

'I want to have a child by you'. That's a marvellous declaration of love between a man and a woman. This certainly is a traditional reason for having children, yet it's still not fundamentally out of date.

I'm not only talking about being physically capable of bringing a child into the world. Being financially and materially capable of bringing it up in good conditions is one of the major considerations in making this choice. Incitement to have children shouldn't still have to be mixed up with social justice.

The socialist government of France and the capitalist government of America make decisions to justify their politics in their own eyes. In France they subject some family allowances to an upper means limit; in America they assist the most disadvantaged households but only allow workers two weeks' official maternity leave and no prenatal leave to pregnant women – two weeks in all! Europeans are much luckier to give birth on this side of the Atlantic! – but these decisions don't do much to improve the downward curve of our populations which are in danger of becoming extinct.

If a bit more market research was done on the family, the necessity would be discovered of 'selling' children to couples who might want them, and that this 'clientele' is currently in a state of transformation.

The most obvious reason for this state is the financial 'favouritism' which benefits women who stop work to bring up a family, together with a general couldn't-care-less attitude towards women who stick to their jobs. These are classic measures which reappear regularly in 'family politics' without necessarily being effective. Most young mothers want to go on working after having a family. They hope that society will both help them to bring up more children and at the same time make it easy for them to continue to lead their double private/working lives, rather than be given a financial incentive to stop working. All the figures for working women prove that that is not what they want from the powers that be: ten years ago 44% of mothers with two children went out to work; today the figure is 64%. With three children, the figure has gone up from 25% to 37%. It goes as high as 67% amongst women in higher social categories!

Measures such as parental leave for two years, unpaid but with *guaranteed re-employment*, or readjustments favouring part-time work, would seem to me much more effective in revitalizing the birthrate than indifferent 'maternity salaries' handed out to women at home which, incidentally are a heavy burden on social budgets. Also, these are not 'fair' measures benefiting as they do primarily those in the most protected sector – qualified civil servants who are more likely than private sector employees to get a good job again after several years of staying at home. And then the most privileged: women whose husbands earn enough money to enable them to lower their own income without endangering the family budget while continuing to pay the mortgage. Sheltered by this favouritism on the part of the birthrate campaigners, they can offer themselves the luxury of having another child.

If the ideas raised in this book sometimes seem too 'elitist' it's not because I've forgotten about the lot of the underprivileged, but because I'm addressing first of all those couples with sufficient income to enable them to plan a bigger family without risk of rocking the boat financially.

It would be quite wrong to preach large families to everyone knowing that for a great many couples this would lead to a financial crisis. Replacing a second salary by a third child hardly helps pay the household bills! On the other hand, it's quite possible to give up a more powerful car or take fewer holidays in order to give your first baby a little brother or sister, or quite simply branch out into a third because you've had so much fun with the first two.

Whether you like it or not, if we want to have more babies, it's necessary to convince managers before staff, professionals before workers and young women graduates before those without qualifications – hoping that later on, when there is less unemployment there will be more women going to university who will choose to think of babies as gifts rather than burdens.

Is that optimistic? But you have to be optimistic to have children and advise others to follow your example as I'm doing. Don't say that our culture has become so pessimistic that it can't offer itself a future?

Kids bore everyone to death

Not only are young adults not in contact with children in their home environment or their everyday lives, but it's as though the childish world is absent from our culture. In the summer of 1985 passers-by in Paris were rather taken aback by a poster campaign whose theme appeared extremely strange to them. The posters showed lots of large, splendid, smiling babies' faces with amusing captions such as: 'Do I look like a government decree?' 'It seems I'm a socio-cultural phenomenon!' Unusual babies who actually weren't trying to sell gold jewellery or skin cream so gentle that even mothers can use it, but only to make you think longingly, to provoke a rush of tenderness and to awaken that powerful desire for a child which comes from heaven knows where. Unfortunately, by the beginning of the autumn term these posters had been taken down, and I had to admit to myself that there wasn't exactly a stampede for the maternity hospitals nine months later. One month's campaign isn't enough to change people's minds!

Our information and communication network is curious about everything, but virtually never gets its cameras rolling in front of cradles or in playgrounds. Television is always expanding its children's programmes, both present and future, but it never speaks to parents as such.

Fully confident that it would have a great success with young parents in many Western countries, I suggested to a programme co-ordinator I knew a monthly series on infant care to incorporate pediatrics and infant psychology and teaching, but she turned me down flat with:

'No, kids bore everyone to death!'

At the same time, there are no less than four regular animal programmes on French television, three in Britain, three in Finland, etc. The result of this is that there are about 16 million cats and dogs in Britain to 6½ million children under ten.

Two cats and dogs for one child. Don't you find that rather a lot? Does this connection between children and pets shock you? However, it does shed a remarkable amount of light on the attitude of society towards what sociologists call 'emotional consumer goods'. Doggies, pussies and little kiddies can all be placed in the top category.

'Emotional consumer goods'

The first time I came across this expression I was quite horrified. Children aren't products that one acquires, possesses and uses to satisfy a need or a whim. A dog maybe, but not a child. Then, on reflection, I found this concept basically accurate. Most people keep a pet for the pleasure of loving it and making it love them in return. How many are responding to the same motivation when they choose to become parents? Especially when they have an only child which they consider the perfect remedy for loneliness (theirs, certainly, not necessarily the child's!).

Even though everyone admits they need live 'emotional consumer goods' to stir up their emotions, why are they so infatuated by four-footed models and so unenthusiastic about manufacturing, running, driving, and then teaching their personal models to stand on their own two feet?

When you compare the advantages and disadvantages of one and the other, you very soon notice that pets fit much more easily into our busy, city-dwellers' lives than children.

Speaking personally, much as I love both categories of creatures, I've had more children than dogs in my life. Yet, as a writer I've noticed that in the last fifteen years authors have without doubt published more books on their love of cats and dogs than of children. Particularly male authors I might add! We will come back to men's loss of fatherly feelings – a phenomenon which is just as significant as women's reluctance to become prolific mothers. Before going on to resolutely serious matters, let's have a little pause to make a puppy/baby and dogs/children comparison. Sometimes, if not always, humour allows for light-hearted observations rather than sanctimonious, pompous statements.

By the way, have you noticed, babies' arrivals are no longer greeted with sighs or resignation. If you want to 'order' one, you need to be happy, good-natured and have a sense of humour. Did you know that this is a very recent phenomenon? In the old days, two babies out of three were more or less considered disasters. Today, two out of three are welcomed with a smile. Most gentlemen who concern themselves with the birthrate seem to have missed this. Perhaps they are too marked by their 'pre-contraception' youth . . . or are they just too solemn?

But that's another story: let's stick to our dogs.

II

Dogs And Babies:
A Comparative Study

Susan is the owner of three superb huskies. Being good sledge dogs, they need to run for more than an hour each day to preserve their health and physique. In the right season, she has no problem. Her work in a ski resort allows her to reconcile her professional life with her canine maternal duties. During the in-between seasons (spring and autumn) things get more complicated, and Susan has to take boring, badly paid jobs so that she can stay where her dogs are happy. The other seasonal workers go off to the seaside or indulge themselves with a bit of city life after three hard months dealing with tourists, without Sundays or weekends. Susan stays in the mountains. Who would want to look after three dogs? Especially sprinters.

Susan doesn't have any children. I've often thought she was more tied to her dogs than she would be to a family.

She's not the only one in that position. I know dozens of couples who 'replace' children with pets. Not households of little old people with no-one to love at home – young couples between twenty-five and thirty! Each one puzzles me and makes me feel a bit sad. Absolutely right to keep your freedom as a young couple before accepting the restraints and responsibilities of parenthood – but then why go and tie yourself up with a dog's lead?

Dogs need to be fed, pampered, taken for walks, cared for, watched over and trained, just like children. They cry when they are left alone just like children, and they are capable of vast amounts of affection but demand an equal amount in return, just like children. As to freedom, there's not much difference between 'train to office/back to doggie' or 'train to office/back to kiddie'. And no-one's going to tell me that a puppy is anything like the same sort of wedding- or living-together-present as a baby.

It wouldn't be so bad if young couples would only choose pocket-size models, such as dachshunds or Yorkshire terriers, but not at all: the craze is for large ones, often very large. Old English sheepdogs, Afghan hounds, dear old Labradors, Pyrenean shepherd dogs, Alsations and anything else you can think of. The sort of dog that takes up the whole back seat of the car, or gets in the way of the kitchen door as he sprawls over the entire floor space of a tiny studio flat – and eats enough for four.

Inevitably, before cluttering up their lives with such an encumbrance, a young couple must have made the choice: 'puppy, not baby'. Doubtless they didn't give enough thought to the advantages and disadvantages of one and the other. Very often, getting a puppy is the result of impulse-buying, whereas these days, with progress in birth control, having a baby implies a mature, considered decision. To enable a couple to make an informed choice, I thought it would be a good idea to carry out a comparative study:-

1. Choosing your model

Looks: Choosing your model of an ideal dog is easier than having to rely on how your baby will turn out. At least, as things are at present! A baby's arrival is the result of a blind order, without guarantee. Genetics being a gamble, it is liable to inherit an unfortunate nose from the in-laws rather than the delicate features of a favourite grandmother. (Haven't you noticed that it's nearly always the in-laws' family that has the reputation of passing on its less than perfect looks?) On the other hand, puppies born 'on the wrong side of the blanket' are much more obviously so than babies, the canine '57 Varieties' rendering crosses aesthetically risky, whereas a mixture of blonde and dark, large and small etc, often improves the quality of babies. There's another, even more serious drawback: with dogs, when a particular breed is in fashion there's an increase in inbreeding, resulting in degeneracy and malformations which only show up as they grow bigger.

Character: A puppy can't produce any guarantee in this department. The pedigree certifies his forbears' physical qualities but not his intelligence, character or ability to adapt to the life planned for him.

As to babies, they seem to present less of a risk. In general the intellectual abilities and characteristics of one or other parent are known before the baby is embarked upon. If you decide to have a baby with someone, it generally means you think highly enough of your partner to take the risk of the baby being like him. Although it's not always an ideal solution to produce a child exactly like yourself, it's unusual not to wish to do so, either secretly or openly.

The only circumstances in which the intellectual faculties of dogs and babies would be a matter of equal guesswork would be in the case of adoption or artificial insemination. As these represent such a minute statistical figure, the best attitude to take is to persuade yourself that 'nothing is inborn, everything is acquired'.

Practicalities: A baby costs nothing to buy – they even pay you a maternity allowance for having him! On the other hand, you can count on between £100 and £300 for a pedigree puppy. You can opt for a male or a female when choosing a dog while you (still) have to leave it entirely to the most dynamic sperm to determine the sex of the baby.

The desire for a puppy can be satisfied almost at once, while the delivery date for all models of babies is around nine months, without taking into account that you can't always put in your order for a particular month – fertilization doesn't succeed every time.

Nevertheless, once the 'model' has been achieved, a

child is much more rewarding than a dog. There's a difference in the way they're acquired: you're proud of something you've created yourself, while you can only be satisfied with a good buy. The 'home-produced' child always beats the 'foreign-made' puppy.

2. Daily routine

People's daily routine and standard of living are much less disrupted by a dog than by a child. At least, that's what they tell us although it's not always obvious.

On the food front: A draw. You have to plan meals and a special diet for both of them. Preparing a baby's meal is hardly more complicated since both little dishes look like a dog's dinner – practically the only difference being that babies eat with a spoon.

A magazine had the amusing idea of comparing the annual food consumption of a twelve-month old baby with that of a medium sized dog weighing 13 kilos.

I've worked out the expenditure for each extra mouth, and it comes to a difference of £300 per annum. A bit more if you give the dog the most expensive tins instead of leftovers; a bit less if you stuff him full of dry biscuits, but I don't know any faithful friends who would put up with nothing but biscuits!

£25 difference per month in the food budget – not much of a reason to reject the baby!

On the clothing front: Advantage dog. It's not often that he needs clothes, whereas not only does a baby have to be dressed, but he spends most of his childhood systematically ruining all his clothes, particularly his shoes.

On the health front: Advantage baby. Puppies and babies are equally likely to be constantly ill. They are regularly sick, have hot noses/cheeks, need to be inoculated against a myriad threatening diseases, grizzle when cutting their teeth and need to be stuffed full of calcium and vitamins to make them grow up strong and healthy.

The baby's overwhelming superiority lies in the fact that he gets free medical treatment under the National Health Service.

The puppy, on the other hand, costs a fortune. Visits to the vet and medicines, three-quarters of which he spits out because you don't know how to give them to him properly, have got to be paid for entirely by the owner! The majority of 'dog fanciers' have no idea what a puppy's health will cost during their first six months of ownership, even when to all appearances he is pretty healthy. It's all right if they get him from a reliable breeder who has produced a robust, properly inoculated specimen. If not, they will spend their whole lives going to the vet and the chemist. They soon find out how their expenses have been inflated thanks to veterinary patent medicines! The sale of baby milk and cereals has gone down in tandem with the birthrate, but the sale of worm powders and flea baths has gone up astronomically.

An insurance company has had the clever idea of setting up health insurance for dogs. The business will undoubtedly recruit its clients from among first-time puppy owners!

On the finance front: Game, set and match to the dog. We have just seen that the dog is heavier, financially speaking, than the baby during its first year of life. On the other hand, the older it gets the less it costs.

The child is quite the opposite: the older it gets the more it costs because mouths to feed put less of a strain on modern family budgets than feet to be shod, homes to be heated, free time to be organized, baby-sitters to be found and school fees to be paid. Babies of carrycot dimensions can't sleep in the sitting room or their parents' bedroom for ever. First-size baby clothes last a month and if you think of this stage until adolescent jeans, expenditure is continual, inexhaustible, essential and unavoidable, even when it seems excessive.

That's without mentioning the upward spiral of pocket money or the bottomless pit of sports gear! Dogs don't buy Smarties and don't need to wear trainers for running! There's good boys!

Finally, once they're grown up dogs don't need subsidized rents, never learn to drive a motor bike or car, or even a moped, and can't open a Post Office savings account at thirteen or fourteen. When they have a family (with their owner's approval) their puppies can sometimes be sold for a good price. Is there any need to point out that the next generation's babies are more an expense than a source of revenue for the grandparents?

3. Upbringing and training

The training period: A child's upbringing and training go on much longer than a dog's. At least fifteen years compared with one at the most. Everyone agrees that the human offspring is the worst finished off product of any living species. He can't walk or get his own food, and the only way he can let you know what he wants and draw everyone's attention to his distress is by yelling at the top of his voice. This is certainly effective, although particularly unpleasant to the ear, especially when you are woken up in the middle of the night.

In fact, the baby needs to be looked after for a very long time if he is to survive. The puppy becomes independent in a few weeks or months as far as being able to move around and eat unaided is concerned.

On the other hand, it's easier to find a keeper for the baby than for the puppy. Most grannies are quite happy to have their Sundays messed up if it's a question of looking after their grandchild, but there aren't many who would be prepared to sacrifice their fitted carpets for the sake of giving their children the weekend off from their still un-housetrained puppy.

Training methods: Puppy training has always been basic – a pat when he's good and obedient and a little smack when he forgets himself in the house or does something naughty.

Conversely such methods which have been handed down over the years, and are nothing more than understandable human reflexes – let anyone who has never smacked a naughty child fling at me the first manual on child care that comes to hand – have been strongly advised against since modern psychology revealed the dangers of frustrations accumulated during early childhood. Ever since then it's been impossible to give a child a slap without feeling guilty, which has greatly improved life for kids, but has enormously complicated the task of those in charge of them, particularly the parents. Explaining and persuading take up much much more time than being insistent and forceful.

Behavioural training therefore seems easier with a puppy. It doesn't last as long, generally gives reliable results and doesn't entail any particular rebellion by the party involved. Quite the reverse – a well trained dog appears proud and grateful to have been put through his apprenticeship and seems to benefit as much as his master from the progress he has achieved.

The child shows far less good will. He demands to know the point of what you're teaching him, and is anti-establishment which doesn't simplify matters during the years when he's learning to get on with the rest of society. It has to be admitted that parents' expectations vis-à-vis their children are much higher than vis-à-vis their dogs. Have you ever heard of a dog reading, writing, qualifying for tennis tournaments, playing the violin nicely or trying to get into medical school?

This is because of the difference in intellectual capacity between children and dogs. The former are blessed with intelligence whereas the latter only have limited instincts which make them do what we expect of them and which we prefer to call 'intelligence'.

Babies are not at all *like* dogs. They are much worse to bring up because they argue, remonstrate, create and have a capacity for causing havoc in everyday life which dogs entirely lack.

On the other hand, children have fantastic brains which astonish everyone who has anything to do with them. Animals' so-called 'intelligence' is nothing but a pale imitation of the faculties of human beings. This is proved by the fact that only babies laugh and have a sense of humour.

I can't think of anything more lovely than a baby's laugh, or his demand for fun when he eggs you on to do whatever it is that gives him great joy – a joy you just have to share. Long before he can talk he understands the joke by his look, his hands and his whole body. I could go on playing 'Peep bo!' for ever when I see those little watchful eyes shining with expectant laughter. That marvellous belly-laugh, anticipating the comic situation every time it's repeated – the laugh which is a memory of the previous one. Laughing with your child or children – with *all* children is an absolute revelation of the profound meaning of life.

Dogs don't know how to laugh – they can't, they're only animals.

No doubt I shall receive some furious letters from animal protection societies and others – I don't care. No-one will ever make me believe that animals are like humans with a bit added on here, a bit taken off there. Konrad Lorenz devoted a large part of his work to showing us the similarities between goslings and our own offspring without convincing me of the anthropological formation of those webfooted creatures.

General assessment of upbringing: Most people are satisfied with the results achieved when their dog reaches maturity. On the contrary, it's more and more unusual these days to come across parents who are proud of the way they have brought up their children. Even if sometimes they have the nerve to show signs of complacency, there are plenty of people around such as teachers, media-men and particularly the children themselves, to put them firmly in their place, in line with the basic theory of psychoanalysis that whatever parents do is bound to turn out wrong. Certain veterinary schools tend to disseminate similar theories – dogs' neuroses are brought on by their masters' mistakes –

but those in charge of upbringing are more resistant to such accusations than those in charge of education.

The fact still remains that, even if the general assessment of upbringing is rarely perfect at the end of the day, the years during which the brain, character and personality are formed and developed are infinitely more full of experiences, communication, creativity and interrelations with children than with dogs. Finally, I would like to add, to the advantage of the child, the notion of durability. To be able to hand on, through the children's upbringing, your knowledge, scale of values, feeling for something or pleasure, is a way of not allowing what you yourself have learnt or acquired to be lost. If there are no children to hand things on to, everything becomes pointless. There's something comforting about not being the last link in the chain.

Sport is a typical example of the urge to hand something on. Keep-fit and tennis enthusiasts know only too well that in time their hearts will beat less energetically and their movements will slow down. To make up for this, I strongly recommend that they transfer their personal ambition to someone younger – a son or a daughter, it doesn't matter which.

I've had this experience myself with skiing which I've always been mad about. Putting my sons on their first skis, watching their progress over the years, feeling full of pride at all their medals, letting them overtake me and admitting that they ski much better than I do (though, of course, there have been such advances in techniques and equipment!) – has all made me forget my own breathlessness and the fact that my style is going more rapidly downhill than I am. Thanks to a mixture of pride and parental love, your own children's performances are the only ones not to make you feel demoralized when they occur at your expense.

4. Emotional relationships

Anything to do with the emotions is essentially subjective and can't be quantified. Putting a price on what you give and receive depends on what you expect to get out of a relationship. Why do certain horrible little lapdogs fill their owners with pride and tenderness as, teeth bared, they attack anything on four feet that has the effrontery to venture on to their territory, while their owners gaze at them in adoration? Why do irresistible three-or four-year-olds irritate their mothers so much when they run up to them, arms outstretched, for a hug when they're not in the mood to give them one?

No objective score, then, just a few common-sense observations.

At birth: The very first weeks aren't much fun with either puppies or new-born babies. However, the fact of having carried it for nine months and the fragility and total dependence of a tiny baby which, in contrast to a puppy, will take months before it can move around on its own, generally makes a baby much more touching – for the mother anyway. Some fathers seem more polite than moved by the sight of this larva which has just entered their lives for life.

Babies: Little balls of fluff and plump little babies are irresistible – most Western adults find them equally so, and those who don't need to be pitied; they are missing one of the purest and most tender moments to be experienced during a human lifetime. Although some historians may have clearly demonstrated that this attraction for tiny babies is a relatively recent cultural acquisition, I find it difficult to believe.

After that stage, however, there's a much greater differential in expectations. Dogs are forgiven a lot, bearing in mind their limitations; much is demanded of children, requiring them to have no limitations. Children can thus give immense satisfaction or terrible disappointment.

That's not the case with dogs. They only need to be good in order to be nice. We've all heard 'doggie–parents' admit with a smile 'My dog's really stupid, but he's so nice!'

You can hardly imagine a mother or father making the same remark about one of their children, even if he's not publicly renowned to be an Einstein.

Childhood and adolescence: This is where the real difference lies, in the length of time involved. A dog remains a puppy for barely a year, just long enough to chew up a few slippers or table legs, run away a few times, for which he's quickly forgiven, and learn not to ruin the carpets by piddling all over them. It certainly isn't the most idyllic period in canine/human relations, but it passes so quickly that on the whole it becomes an amusing memory.

As for children, they never seem to finish growing up. Losing their charm and innocence bit by bit over the years, they end up thoroughly complicating relationships when at the hellish pinnacle of their adolescence and post-adolescence. Viewed from outside, the goal of their machinations appears to consist entirely of wrecking the emotional relationship with their parents in order to arrive at a final detachment which will prove to them that they have become adults. It's only when they've passed this peak that they can at last become nice again – pleasant to live with, and sometimes even considerate.

Adults: At this stage, the situation is clear – dogs remain faithful till death no matter what happens. Children get more and more detached till death, no matter what happens. And the amazing thing is that parents don't just admit this is so, but actually encourage it, because children who are too attached run the risk of not building a sufficiently full and independent life for themselves.

That's why, logically, young people ought to have children – to get the largest possible amount of pleasure out of them while they still can.

As for those who are no longer young, they are absolutely right to take comfort in dogs when they no longer enjoy the privileged relationship which can only be shared with their children for a few years.

So isn't the world turning rather upside-down when

there are young people who have dogs, and old people who have regrets that they didn't experience the joys of parenthood while there was still time?

5. Social value

There's one last item to add to the score for the 'dogs versus children' match; social relationships. On this point, dogs are indisputably superior. Pets fit into present-day routines much more easily than small children.

To be persuaded of this you only have to carry out the following experiment: during a Sunday afternoon walk, try to have a conversation with ten strangers: five dog owners and five mothers or fathers with a child under seven. If you ask the dog owner about his pet's breed, age or character, taking care that you embark on the conversation with a friendly 'What a beautiful dog!' or 'What a handsome expression your dog has' . . . apart from a few very exceptional cases of aggressiveness – watch out for Doberman owners who don't exactly glow with friendliness – you will get five detailed, friendly replies as starting off points for a long conversation. In a few minutes you will be familiar with the dog's entire family tree: 'He's my third terrier. When you've got to know these sort of dogs, you can't imagine having any other kind . . .'

If you dare to show this sort of familiarity towards a strange child, the grown-ups with him will frown disapprovingly. They're so unused to people taking an interest in children that they're suspicious of absolutely anyone who tries to be friendly. If you say tentatively 'What a dear little baby – is it a boy or a girl?' or 'How old is he?' they cut you dead with the kind of look that tells you they're wondering whether you're a sexual deviant, a kidnapper or just a talkative bore who will grab any pretext to get into conversation. If, unfortunately, you accompany your remarks with a big, tender smile they mutter something unintelligible, turn pointedly on their heels and push the pram away, saying to the baby 'Come along, darling, we're going home'!

This happens to me all the time because I love small children in the same way that other people love dogs. Not only when they're mine – I also get the greatest pleasure out of watching other people's children. I find their playful antics more fascinating than those of any animal in the world. So I get regular black looks when I talk to them without previous permission from the grown-up in charge.

A society out of touch with children

Sadly, we live in an atomized, urbanized, cloistered society whose children are the personal, exclusive property of their parents even if that means suffocating them beneath the weight of their parents' presence and responsibility – items which they are able to share less and less often.

In villages in the old days, children, like dogs, roamed free. Each member of the community knew them, and would speak to them and ask them in for a sweet when they had the chance. Nowadays dogs and children are kept indoors in the name of safety and little by little the community is forgetting the delights of street life which have given way to uncivilized traffic noise. Children are rather a nuisance because of their impulsiveness, their slowness, their inexperience – their specific biological rhythms upset the fast pace lived at by modern city dwellers. The other day an angry motorist next to me in a traffic jam was furiously revving his engine to try and hurry up a little six- or seven-year old who was crossing on the zebra in front of his bonnet!

So much so that parents with several children are no longer considered lucky, courageous, generous or optimistic, but rather as irresponsible people who don't only complicate their own lives, but irritate innocent citizens, less feckless than themselves, with their horde of children. Take a look at travellers' pained expressions when a child cries in a railway carriage or on board are under five feet six, eat nothing but chicken and chips, don't drink wine, get under the waiters' feet and send up the decibels but not the bills.

A headhunter confided in me the other day that, on being given the task of flushing out a dynamic young executive, the would-be employer had made a point of saying: 'Between ourselves, I prefer young men who are keen on sport because they are less frequently ill, married because they are less likely to run after girls during working hours and fathers of one or two children, not more. Above all not more than two otherwise they don't take home so many files at the weekend and spend the whole time talking about their kids, which I fine supremely irritating'.

Mothers already suffer from professional ostracism. Now it seems that fathers too are in danger of becoming victims of the current war against parenthood!

III

Parenthood Is No Longer What It Was

Everyone would like to be part of a vast 'clan' with its emotional ties, childhood memories and mutual assistance. It's the surest remedy against loneliness, the ups and downs of professional life and the disappointments of married life. This family has its (family) house, its (family) celebrations, its (family) spirit, its (family) recipes and (family) objects, traditions and jokes. Sociologists all confirm that its value is increasing and that there is more and more need for it.

The problem is that everyone would like to live surrounded by the largest family possible while they themselves have the smallest family possible. Their ideal is to be a strictly nuclear family – Mum/Dad/Boy/Girl, but with plenty of cousins, nephews, etc. In twenty years, from 1962–1982, households with four children under twenty-five have decreased by a third; conversely, couples with one child have increased by a quarter.

Parenthood on a large scale can no longer be regarded as a reference point for parents to identify or compare themselves with. It is no longer an ideal to be achieved, but instead has become a rather outdated option amongst the many and varied life styles which proliferate in Western societies. As time goes on, it gets further and further away from our way of life. The number of people living alone has doubled in twenty years; it's tripled in Switzerland and even quadrupled in Canada. In France, one-parent families already represent one-third of the total which is difficult to believe, but this figure nevertheless corresponds with the statistics of bachelors, unofficial mistresses, those who are separated and divorced, widows and widowers. Their proportion rises continually.

What we called the 'me generation' in the seventies still hasn't completely digested its frenzied dose of individualism. You only need to take a good look round to realize that for the last fifteen years the whole media and cultural environment has ignored children, or even obliterated them.

The current image of a woman illustrates this voluntary amnesia. Fashion demands a supple, elongated look with narrow hips, girlish breasts, flat stomach and an athlete's thighs – a unisex body which is in danger of losing its perfection with the first pregnancy. Aesthetic terrorism has become an obsession. I wonder how many young women anxiously consult their bathroom scales each day when they're expecting a baby, to make sure there's no danger of them changing into an 'earth-mother' the day after they've given birth! Some lucky ones get their figures back, but most of them find themselves young mothers with a baby *plus* several extra pounds to worry about. Dear Rubens, Renoir and Matisse, your roly-poly ladies have aged a lot more than your talent, which has survived the years without a wrinkle!

All the doctors reckon that the main worry of expectant mothers is the selfish fear of what childbirth will do to their figures. This comes way in front of the normal worry of producing an abnormal child, which is still present though much reduced by the progress of modern medicine.

The first one: an essential ritual

The first baby still makes it – he represents a sort of essential ritual which is needed to gratify a certain amount of self-seeking, to reassess the many-sided aspect of the human condition and to ensure full integration in a society where hyper-fertility is by no means rated highly, but where sterility suggests a kind of abnormality. An only child certifies that you are in good physical working order and avoids the question: But why haven't he, she or they got any children?'

I got the feeling I had made a terrible faux pas when, having just met a woman of about thirty-five who told me she was having to move to the capital from the country, I asked her 'What are you going to do about the children's school if you're moving house in the middle of the year?' She blushed violently, replying that she hadn't got any children and immediately explained this deficiency by telling me, without being asked – that she and her husband hadn't been able to have any and that she was dying to adopt some, but her husband had absolutely no desire to do so. . . .

All embarrassed, I first of all put on a stupid, sad expression when she told me she couldn't have children, and then tried to look cheerful as I congratulated her on the freedom she could benefit from, both in her professional life and in her choice of where she wanted to live. It all sounded false and she was upset.

No, it's not easy living in our sort of society when you're over thirty-five and have no children at all. Apart from 19% of couples who are physically sterile, you find very few who have made a conscious decision not to have children. In answer to the question 'How many children would you like, or would have liked to have?' only 4% of men and women reply 'None'. The majority want to have one or two (51%). The others long for bigger families (three or four children) but they won't actually have them. All the experts know that the 'ideal size' and the 'real size' of a family never coincide. The longing is always greater than reality. One child is fine, two are all right, but three – that's when the trouble starts!

A large family is like marital fidelity – everyone is for it, but few are capable of carrying it through. When you ask people 'Are you in favour of marital fidelity?' the majority reply with an overwhelming, well-meant YES. Does this mean that the majority of our contemporaries are over-whelmingly virtuous?

Substantial rather than large

We definitely should find a different expression from 'large family' with its negative implications, conjuring up as it does: couples who in the old days brought up masses of children in precarious financial circumstances; over-crowded dwellings; mothers deformed by constant pregnancies and breast feeding; deserving fathers, staggering under the burden of hordes of children; old clothes distributed by charities; girls without qualifications sent into service; boys joining up under age to lighten the family burden; neglected teeth and unkempt hair.

Even we ourselves, the 'baby-boom' mothers of the fifties who often brought up three or four children, never wanted to be known as 'mothers of large families'. On the contrary, we considered it a challenge to bring up several children and at the same time preserve our personalities as women better than our mothers had – we refused to give ourselves up totally to motherhood.

If the expression 'great family' wasn't confined to the aristocracy and a few privileged people with wealth or power, it would be much more suitable than 'large'. This idea of status sounds good and is less derogatory. A large family doesn't only represent more mouths to feed and beds to make, it equally implies diversity, a wealth of individual experiences and relationships, generosity in everyday life and, obviously, more fun. When I questioned mothers and fathers while preparing this book, I never heard the words 'large family' used to describe an indi-vidual situation. 'We have three children', 'I have two boys and a girl', 'I am mother/father of an enormous brood . . . of a great gang . . . of four little things, of three devils'. I heard everything except 'large family'. This only came up in connection with general observations on the difficulties in life or the loss of spending money which threatens those who don't control their families.

We're going to have to think up a new expression to describe a notion which has had a very bad name since the 19th century. The middle classes realized that dividing their money up by two instead of four or five or, preferably, not dividing it up at all but handing it down to a sole descendant, gave them a better chance of making their fortune!

However, nowadays, three or four children don't entail systematic impoverishment of the parental home, mainly because the standard of living in Western nations has risen by 53% in twenty years at the exact moment when families in Europe, as in North America, have been at their largest following the baby boom of the fifties.

Young people who are between twenty-five and forty today have twice as many brothers and sisters as their children will have, and yet they don't appear to have suffered from privation or misery during their childhood. In the developed countries they have never lacked necessities, or even in many cases, luxuries.

In spite of that, for the last twenty years we have been surrounded by images and archetypes that have been inspired by self-cultivation, individual freedom and professional success. In this sort of culture, there's no place for family units which are larger than average.

In political discussion, children imply conservative thinking

On the left, a high birthrate has had a bad name since the 19th century. It is considered a sign of the most reactionary conservatism. Who was it that used to demand children from the people?

- Warmongers, to endow their country with a large army, an inexhaustible supply of cannon fodder. Mussolini and Khomeini, what's the difference?
- Priests, against any form of contraception because of their respect for life but also because of their belief in sexual repression for moral reasons. Since gratification of the flesh is a sin, its only 'excuse' is its necessity for reproduction.

In countries like Ireland, Canada and the United States, the stand taken by the Catholic church in support of a high birthrate proved itself to be effective from a demographic point of view in the first half of the 20th century. Little by little the Catholic minority gained in significance and influence faced with the less prolific Protestant community. Nowadays religious fantaticism still guarantees demographic expansion in Muslim countries. The influence of the church, as well as being a pillar of resistance to Moscow, also ensures an exceptional population growth amongst the Poles.

    – Capitalists – fat cigar between their teeth! – a high birthrate amongst the most under-privileged classes provided them with a workforce that was both prolific and cheap.

Where were the largest families to be found? Right at the bottom of the social ladder among the least educated who continued to breed without control. With each baby the family's means were reduced and their chances of escaping from their predicament were lessened. In the old days the countryside was inhabited by an impoverished, underpaid workforce consisting of young farm labourers, both boys and girls, whose parents, unable to support them, had placed them there as soon as they reached adolescence.

At the time of the exodus from the countryside in Europe, as in the United States, children of large families migrated with their parents to the towns. The only thing to do was to put them to work in the factories at a very early age for wretched wages. They provided the 'moneyed' classes with their fat bank accounts. Pacifists, laymen and socialists by tradition, the left were bound to be mistrustful. Until the middle of the 20th century, they had a horror of anything to do with the birthrate debate, which they associated with all forms of fascism.

Then followed the struggle for Women's Lib, demands for sex equality at work and the abortion debate. Each time the conservatives want to preserve the status quo – each time the left wants to be innovative, reformative or revolutionary. Their positions get further and further apart.

In all Western countries, young people are more often attracted to ideas 'of the left' than they are to conservative ideologies. At the same time, it's the thirty- to thirty-five-year olds who make the decisions concerning the size of the family. QED: the political argument which has the most impact on men and women of childbearing age is the one that stresses the advantages of individualism and freedom, and completely ignores the joys of family life.

It is only very recently in a country like France that a left wing President has dared to point out the need for encouraging and supporting parents with more than two children. A socialist minister, braving the sarcasm of her fellow-politicians, was courageous enough to declare in the press:

> 'If we want a strong France, with a responsible population, solidarity and independence are absolutely indispensable qualities.
>
> I believe that a large family has a better capacity to integrate into society than a small family. I also believe that in a family with several children each of its members has a larger capacity for independence. Large families are important for French society. However, that is not current thinking – it is considered more usual to have small families.'

By quite a coincidence the minister referred to is a woman and mother of four.

The French left displayed quite an avant-garde attitude by allowing such a declaration to be published under a socialist signature. The German Greens, the American radicals and the Nordic social democrats have none of them reached such a turning-point. In Spain and Italy which were more deeply affected by their years of fascism, where women feel they have only too recently thrown off the yoke of an interfering, all-powerful clergy, a policy for increasing the birthrate is still unpopular. Over there, babies are still wrapped in white shawls – they're not supposed to be born brandishing a tiny pink wrist.

Financially speaking, children are a heavy investment

A child is no longer an eventual source of revenue as he was in the past; he is more likely to be the cause of unavoidable expenditure. Not wanting to relinquish the comfortable habits he's been used to since childhood, and because of extended studies and unemployment, the years during which a child is dependent on his family go on growing longer and longer. The more the parents' standard of living goes up, the more material demands the children make on them.

I've had hundreds of discussions on this subject with European parents – about the next generation's insatiable need for money. We came to the conclusion that our own way of living, means of transport and pursuit of leisure were no longer luxuries, but had become facts of life and an example for our children.

For instance, let's look at the fantastic expansion in leisure. The parents of today's young adults were the first to benefit from it. They took their children on holiday abroad with them as a matter of course. (We wouldn't have dreamt of leaving our kids at home while we were skiing or sunbathing – our guilty consciences would have ruined most of our pleasure!) What was new to us at twenty or thirty became routine to them from an early age. Therefore it's nothing out of the ordinary for English, German, Swedish or Dutch young people to spend several weeks a year in a sunny country. Some students from places like London, Paris or Milan consider a week's skiing each year an essential minimum if they are to avoid a nervous depression during the dark days of winter. Most American or Canadian 'juniors' are quite unable to imagine how to get around without a car, or travel more than 500 miles without an airline ticket. They all swear that as soon as it's their turn to be parents they will make sure their children splash about in a warm sea when they're hardly out of the cradle.

They can't see themselves building a nest if it means having to give up these family pastimes which are as much part of their necessities of life as hot running water or the telephone.

When they – rather belatedly – tot up how much they have cost their own parents, young adults hesitate before entering into a parental contract with its heavy financial commitments and its evermore indeterminate length. If they wait to become parents themselves until they enjoy the same standard of living as was provided for them by their parents at the end of their working lives, they will be long in the tooth before their babies have even started cutting theirs!

If the present trend to prolong post-adolescence indefinitely continues and accelerates in years to come, shall we see young men and women in the 21st century celebrating their thirtieth birthdays at home with Mummy and Daddy? The idea may be laughable, but at the same time it could make those in favour of large families shake in their shoes!

Children don't only cost their parents a lot – they also constitute a heavy investment by the nation, in allowances, pre-, peri- and post-natal care, maternity leave, nurseries, kindergartens, schools, further education, etc. . . . Please don't think this is my view. I'm just expressing the opinion of many tax payers.

Old people cost a lot too, but there's a big difference: the nation can't choose whether or not to take on the responsibility of old people, whereas they can choose not to have children. It's easier not to give someone life than to let someone die. Also, societies when faced with the cost of the elderly have naturally given priority to raising their standard of living, even if it has meant back-pedalling on measures in favour of the family. The alternatives have never been clearly set out, but many democracies have adopted budgetary measures in this general direction. In the last twenty years in France, the share of family allowances in the national budget has decreased, while the sums allocated to sickness and old-age benefits have doubled.

The United States provides another example of this. In

1983 there were four times more children than old people living below the official poverty line. In the Federal Budget of 1983 the total sum allocated to assistance for old people was four times that granted to families.

Sylvia Ann Hewlett, quoting those figures in a book which had a great impact on the other side of the Atlantic, made this heartfelt plea on behalf of mothers who she considers are being passed over in American society today:

> 'It is no secret that old people's standard of living has improved considerably in the last few years because they are well organized and have learnt how to use their electoral power to obtain measures in their favour from politicians. American parents would do well to arm themselves accordingly.'

One can always see the mote in the eye of a neighbouring country's policies, but very rarely the beam in the eye of one's own financial decisions. Honestly, what democratic government of today would dare to deprive the elderly of spending money in order to hand it over to families?

Children turn our lives upside down

Women know and men dread the fact that children turn our lives upside down. A young father pointed out rather wistfully:

'A child represents the transition from couple to family. What man doesn't at that time dread the thought of giving up his youthful freedom? From that moment on, he's an adult.'

When there's only one child, parents more or less manage by fitting him into their lives, or dumping him on other good-natured adults. It's most unusual that nurseries, baby-sitters, neighbours, grandmothers, uncles, aunts or girlfriends would refuse to have one child on his own. You take him with you when you go out for the evening or away for weekends or holidays. He's often short of sleep, but not company.

As soon as there are two children, everything changes. The whole world becomes centred round their lives. Instead of making the child fit into an adult routine, the parents have to reorganize their lives to cope with the demands of real family life. If both parents go out to work, which is the case nowadays in most families with two children,[1] organizing a timetable produces endless complications, stress and arguments: 'Can you pick the baby up from the nursery tonight? I've got an appointment with the doctor to find out whether Tom needs to have his adenoids out. Whoever gets home first starts cooking the supper'.

There's no need to dwell on this sort of early morning haggling which takes place between a shower that was too cold and coffee that's too hot; it's a time when children whine and grown-ups grumble. We've all been through it – above all, we've read all about it time and again in our favourite women's magazines.

In order to protect mothers, we journalists who write about everyday matters have had a tendency to write only about the negative and disruptive side of children. What is astonishing and even encouraging is that, in spite of this, so many young couples have decided to accept the responsibility of parenthood. They really must have had a whole-hearted desire for children!

People all but offer their condolences when you announce a third pregnancy either at the office or at home:

'It was incredible' said Margaret, a thirty-five-year-old departmental head in a private company, 'the reactions I got from everyone when I started talking about this third pregnancy! The girls in the office looked as

1. According to a worldwide enquiry, in France 71% of mothers with one child, 60% of mothers with two children, 40% of mothers with three children or more go out to work. We should remember that in the 1975 census 55% of married women with one child, 41% with two children and 23% with three or more went out to work. The figures are even higher in Denmark and England, but with a considerable proportion of mothers working part-time. In contrast, in Holland only 20% of married women work.

dismayed as though I had told them I had a serious illness. They all but said goodbye to me, convinced that the only thing I could do was to stop working.

The boss looked furious, but that's nothing unusual. Every time one of us gets pregnant he wishes he was Japanese, in which case he could sack us without any difficulty as soon as we got married. Curiously enough, he puts up with long sick leaves when his faithful colleagues have had a serious car accident or are suffering from heart trouble, but maternity leave affects him personally as though he was being pickpocketed!

The most amazing thing was our parents' reaction. You'd have thought they would be pleased at being grandparents for a third time. With three children on my side and four on my husband's, you wouldn't think our "fruitfulness" would have dismayed them. Their reaction was quite the opposite, rather in this sort of vein: "In our day it was all right still. Nowadays, with the sort of life you lead it's madness!" – in spite of the fact that my husband and I together earn more than our fathers did with only one breadwinner.

It wouldn't have been so bad if my mother hadn't treated my husband like an irresponsible chauvinist. She had all the difficulty in the world accepting that I had been in full agreement over this child, and had actually wanted it. "My poor darling", she kept sighing, "What a terrible life you're going to have!"

If the child hadn't been the result of so much mature reflection it would have been almost enough to make us decide to have an abortion.'

This is absolutely typical of the prevailing atmosphere. Not only is it no longer usual to want children, but it is considered friendly and kind-hearted to dissuade others from doing so. Such warnings have one great advantage: it becomes impossible later on for parents who have been duly warned to involve you too much in their daily problems. 'I told you so!' is a marvellous let-out when you are asked to be helpful or understanding! Personnel managers in firms where the workforce is mainly female show a masterly use of this method!

Children can be a source of guilt to those bringing them up

How far off are those happy days when children's physical health was the only basis for telling good parents from bad ones. As long as they were well, the main goal had been achieved. Healthy children were a guarantee that they had been well fed, well treated and well loved. If on top of that they were polite, saying 'Good morning' to the lady and 'Thank you' when they were given a sweet, the parents could be proud that they had been so successful.

In our competitive and complicated world the certificates for 'good and loyal service to parenthood' are much more difficult to get. Nowadays for a child to be worthy of his parents he needs to be not only healthy, but also:

Good looking. Looks play an increasingly decisive role in human relationships. You no longer mainly choose a fiancée for her dowry, a husband for his kindness or social position, a business colleague for his qualifications, a secretary for her typing speed or a writer because you like his books. Above all else, they must be pleasant to look at. More than that, they must definitely be good looking. Photography, the cinema and television continually put across idealized images of youth and seduction.

Whereas nothing can be less certain than producing a series of Venuses and Adonises. How can you guarantee the aesthetic quality of a product which you get under production without any real control over its manufacture? And afterwards we parents have to wear ourselves out organizing braces for their teeth, supports for their arches, glasses, getting their ears straightened or paying for dancing and deportment classes without any certain guarantee of the results.

If, as is usually the case, they don't look like Isabelle Adjani or Robert Redford when they get to fifteen, whose fault is it? The parents', of course.

Slim. We still forgive parents if their children don't have perfectly regular features. This 'flaw' can be blamed on some gene or other. But if your child is fat it's no good trying to escape the blame! You've overfed him, stuffed him and ruined him with sweets and dollops of chocolate ice cream, poor little victim of your basic maternal instinct.

I sometimes envy mothers in the old days who had a clear conscience about providing bread and soup, and making or buying puddings to please their brood without counting the calories. They used to boast about their family's appetite and even their greed. Since dieticians have ruled the roost it's quite out of the question to allow oneself to carry on in such an old-fashioned way. Going without pudding is no longer a punishment but a wise precaution.

Even though medical research has revealed the virtues of being slim, it must be admitted that parents have lost a lot of simple pleasure because of it – pleasure which I'm convinced forms part of our nature as mammals. No need to talk about 'sugar-free' children who sadly watch their little friends guzzling sweets without always understanding why they themselves aren't allowed these sticky treats which are in all the shops and are constantly being advertised on the television.

If on top of your steamed vegetables and your fat-free milk products your kids make pigs of themselves on bars of chocolate after lessons, or devour hamburgers and chips in McDonalds opposite their school, ending up 20lbs over-weight when they're grown up, whose fault is it? The parents', naturally.

Bursting with qualifications. When a child fails in his studies, the parents get it in the neck. The trend of psychiatric opinion, and the demands of the job market join forces in terrorizing mothers and fathers whose

children are lazy, poetic, good with their hands or dilet-
tantes.

Japan is typical of this parental conscience. Everything
there is extreme: the obsession with good school and exam
results, and the absolute necessity for a grown-up to be at
home in the evenings to make sure the children do their
homework till a late hour. Surely, like children the world
over, they'd like to hang around doing nothing from time to
time. The results are well documented: Japan has both the
highest percentage of workers with A levels and the record
for teenage suicides. Japanese fathers have discovered the
trick of how to avoid feeling guilty – they have totally off-
loaded this educational responsibility on to their wives. It
seems that this fear of failure at school is a much more
decisive factor in birth control than contraception. How
can you have more than one or two children if each has to
be top of the class?

Also, the Japanese have soothed their consciences
by only attaching inordinate importance to the education
of boys, even though this has meant introducing a
little flexibility into girls' education. In the United States
and Europe, where there is an equal obsession over
scholastic achievement, the failure rate is in danger of being
twice as high, as nowadays girls have to be equally bursting
with qualifications. What's become of the good old days
when you commiserated with a boy for having failed his
exams as you sent him off to see the world before coming to
join Daddy in the family business? Those golden days when
a small dowry was much more likely to ease your
conscience about your daughter's education than a useless
diploma?

These days, for us to be able to regard ourselves
proudly in the mirror when we're examining our wrinkles,
our children must all have degrees in business studies or
engineering. If they have difficulty passing their O levels,
fail their A levels, have no particular vocation and find
themselves on the dole, whose fault is it? The parents',
obviously.

Well balanced and free from complexes. Of all the impossible bets that children's upbringing involves, this one is renowned as the most unattainable. However, it's in this domain that parents are generally considered to be totally responsible.

Psychiatrists everywhere, you have undoubtedly helped some sufferers from neuroses to regain their sleep and their zest for life but, on the other hand, have you thought about the number of mothers and fathers whose sleep you have disturbed and whose strength to bring up their children you have 'sapped'? By explaining to parents that no matter what they do the result will be bad, Freud's disciples have managed to dampen the enthusiasm for their children which enabled parents to teach gestures, relationships and habits as a matter of course.

A paediatrician, Dr Edwige Antier, gave me considerable pleasure when she wrote, on the subject of the falling birthrate:

> 'This psychological fad for parental guilt has created a fear of children which brings back to every mother a mirror-image of all the crises and break-ups in her life.
>
> It doesn't matter whether you divorce, get on badly with your husband or are unable to make ends meet, each time you are the guilty party. Even though everyone passes through difficult periods in their lives.
>
> As soon as there is the slightest problem, everyone is down on the parents. The grandparents defend their own way of doing things with "I've told you so lots of times . . ." Friends are able to soothe their own disappointments by seeing that other people's children also have personality problems. Teachers relieve their consciences by delving into the parents' private lives. Finally, when you go to see professionals such as speech therapists or psychologists, they shoot at you the fatal question "Didn't you yourself have any problems with your parents when you were a child?"
>
> On the other hand, if everyone said to themselves: "But a child is joy personified, he's a continual

question mark, and no-one knows a perfect way of bringing him up" – having children would be much more fun.'

At the present moment we're a long way away from this sympathetic paediatrician's theories. Every time a child suffers from personality problems, complexes, sudden changes of mood, bedwetting, bulimia or anorexia, or simply wants to make life impossible for everyone round him just to make his presence felt, who do you turn to with reproachful looks? It goes without saying – to the parents.

Children have completely disappeared from our cultural environment

The world of contemporary artists no longer contains a Mozart, a Victor Hugo or a Picasso. Modern-day composers, artists and painters have little time for children. Amongst the loves that they write or sing about, film, paint or sculpt, angelic children only have a tiny place. No doubt they're not erotic enough. Children are absent from plays, scripts, and screens both large and small. You no longer see their touching faces or awkward silhouettes when you go to picture exhibitions. Press photographers only let them into the picture to improve their famous parents' image. Can you really count this as being part of our culture?

People no longer sing motherhood's praises either. In art, a woman is never portrayed as more than an object of desire or as narcissistically contemplating her own beauty – she always has an adolescent figure and hints sensually at seduction and pleasure. Pregnancy might coarsen those slim, well-toned bodies; a child might detract these women from their mission in life – to stay beautiful for ever. Stars have always concealed their private lives so they can remain symbols. Can anyone imagine Greta Garbo or Marilyn Monroe playing mother?

How can you explain this disappearance of the mother and child which have inspired so many masterpieces over the centuries? I've discovered two possible causes – neither one stands up on its own, but joined together they can explain our rejection of motherhood and children from our culture.

The first proof: more and more artists are living on the fringe, without a family, babies or schoolchildren to disrupt or enliven their lives. In London as in Rome, in Madrid as in New York, they live among themselves, according to customs and patterns which are unlike our own. Nocturnal, solitary, tormented, they themselves and their work come before everything. They would rather talk about their own childhood, tirelessly searching for the meaning of their lives or their genius than listen to childish babblings or French conjugations. They are really only interested in one mother, and that's their own.

On the other hand, the sexual freedom of the last twenty years, the sudden go-ahead to say everything, show everything and dare everything, have opened up an immense field of inspiration to artists, all of which had been forbidden until then. The representation, description and idolizing of sex, which for a long time had been repressed in their extreme forms, have polarized creative inspiration at the expense of other sources which had been more fully explored. It's no longer necessary to use breast-feeding as an excuse to show 'breasts that can never be seen'.

This cultural blotting-out of childhood doesn't correspond with a loss of affection on the part of the public. On the contrary, when a writer, going against the current trend, chooses a child as hero he can be certain of having a tremendous success.

That's how parents have gradually come round to thinking that having children would be a risk beyond both their means and their capabilities.

The result is clear to see: demographers are witnessing birthrate curves and fertility indicators plunging in a dizzy fashion in all the developed countries. They cry 'wolf' so often that no-one listens to them any more.

IV

Danger Signals For The Year 2000

As we approach the end of the second millennium, our calendars and computers remind us that we must do our accounts – and calculations are going ahead at full speed. The fateful date of the year 2000 endows predictions with a somewhat mystical aspect. The Ancients, not having technological dangers or scientific worries, scared themselves at the approach of the year 1000 by foretelling the end of the world. The bogeyman of modern, computerized nations is the fall in the birthrate.

'Collapse', 'Disaster', 'Breakdown', 'Collective Suicide' are some of the uncompromising expressions used to describe the fall in the birthrate in Western nations. Statisticians all say the same thing:

1. We are not having enough children to ensure the replacement of future generations.
2. At the same time as birthrates are collapsing, the number of deaths is declining, and we shall soon be living in a world of little old people.
3. These two phenomena, when combined, pose considerable sociological, economical and political problems. We are living on the edge of the crisis now, but the real, enormous crisis of global balance between north and south, west and east is only just beginning. Could it be the end of Western civilisation?

Very few of those who study the future dare reply to this last question with a genuine YES. First of all because they know you can never be certain the worst will happen, and also because they have learnt by experience not to trust forecasts. In its collective behaviour the human herd sometimes reacts in strange ways, either by starting to breed again just when it seems to have given up or, caring less about the future than the present, by obstinately refusing to reproduce itself no matter how much it may be urged to do so.

All countries have passed the word around

The French appear the most alarmist. However, their situation is neither unique nor particularly critical compared with other Western countries. All the Western democracies are passing through the same birthrate crisis.

The countries of Eastern Europe aren't having the same problems. The USSR with a birthrate figure of 2.4 children per woman is replacing its population more than adequately, and even expanding it: in five years (1980–1985) her population has increased by ten million inhabitants – thanks, it must be pointed out, to the extraordinary fertility of the Moslem republics. All Communist bloc countries except Hungary and East Germany are still above two. The birthrate champion of the East is Poland, whose unchanging fertility we have already discussed. Lech Walesa, a rebel who has been in and out of prison several times, must be the only trade unionist in the world to carry on the fight while at the same time caring for an ever increasing family – he already has seven children!

Gerard Calot, director of l'Institut d'Etudes Demographiques, points out:

'The situation in France reflects those in Europe, the United States, Canada . . . never before in peacetime has there been such a flagging birthrate. All these countries seem to have passed the word around.

France is relatively healthy compared with her European neighbours. Great Britain, West Germany, Italy, and Switzerland have figures of 1.8 to 1.3 children per woman . . .'

To this list can be added: all the Scandinavian countries, Belgium, Holland, Austria, Japan, Australia and New Zealand. All of them, including France with 1.82 in 1985, are below the famous 2.1 considered indispensable for the 'replacement of the generations'.[1]

1 + 1 = 2.1 Why?

It's odd, this 'point one'. Two children should be enough to replace Mummy and Daddy, but they aren't quite: primary arithmetic doesn't satisfy demographic rules – they have to take into account the conditions that govern the survival of the species. Michel-Louis Levy a French demographer, explains this birthrate rule:

'As they say, it takes two to have a child. Once a couple has brought two children into the world, they can be said to have "replaced" themselves. To ensure replacement of the generations it is obviously necessary for each couple to have two children. It is all right if the replacement is carried out by couples generally – or rather by women generally: therefore, you can have a woman without a child or with only one as long as there are other women with three or more to compensate.

Altogether, replacement of the generations requires that 100 women have 200 children. But as 105 boys are born to every 100 girls, to enable 100 women

1. Note in Appendix I the principal fertility figures of Western countries compared with those of a certain number of under-developed countries as well as the graphs showing comparative population growth in France, Great Britain, the USA, Italy and West Germany.

to have 100 girls they must each have 205 children. In addition, these girls must reach the age of procreation, which is twenty-seven. Unfortunately some die before this age. At the present time, for every 100 girls that are born, two die before they get to twenty-seven. Therefore, to make up for these residual deaths, you need to add about 2% to the original fertility figures: in order that 100 women have 100 girls capable of reproducing they need to have 210 children, not only 205. That equals *2.1 children per woman*.'[2]

Children expressed in decimal points

If all the men and women in the West made an agreement to stick to this figure of 2.1, what would happen? The population would be renewed, that is to say there would be as many young British, French, Japanese and Spaniards in twenty or fifty years' time as those countries' generations contain now. On the contrary, if the birthrate doesn't improve in the next fifteen years, the situation will inevitably deteriorate in the 21st century. Depending on whether the couples of today and the next fifteen years continue reproducing at the same pace, slightly increase the size of their families or decide that they want even less children, the population growth in France will vary considerably from 2020, and still more so from 2040.

A study by I.N.S.E.E. on 'The population of metropolitan France at the beginning of the third millennium' demonstrates clearly by its projections what effect fertility figures can have on the population. They have drawn four hypotheses:

1.5 children per woman. A bit less than the last few years.

2. This figure is necessarily higher in developing countries where lack of hygiene and medical facilities, together with a very low living standard lead to heavy infant mortality. In Europe at the beginning of the century, three children per woman were necessary to replace one generation.

Quite a plausible figure as countries like Finland or West Germany are already below it.

1.8 children per woman. The present level observed in France and also in Great Britain, the United States and Canada.

2.1 children per woman. Figure needed to replace the population.

2.4 children per woman: this would mean a sort of second baby boom, which is hard to believe at the moment, but which could take place nevertheless.

The following table gives projections of the French population in the next fifty years, starting from an estimated 56 million in 1990.

FERTILITY	2000	2020	2040
1.5	56739	54985	48451
1.8	57883	58664	55656
2.1	59114	62589	63799
2.4	60183	66390	72387

Incredible differences! With children expressed in decimal points – a perfectly barbaric though scientifically accurate notion! – the variations in rise and fall of the population over half a century can be numbered in tens of millions.

We are used to manipulating figures for the East, or South America, but we hardly ever juggle around with our own population figures. Perhaps because of our craze for individualism, we still refuse to see that our personal decisions can have any effect on the future of the nation.

We may wonder if it really matters all that much whether there are 10 million more or less French, British and Italians, or whether they've reached 350 million in the States or have only just scraped over the 300 million mark. Would that really change the balance of power and the economic and cultural influence of these countries? A nation's power comes from the quality of its brains not the quantity of its brawn. Peaceful, cunning little countries with populations of less than 10 million live very well, and sometimes even better than once-large ones. Switzerland and Sweden occupy enviable little slots in the company of nations.

In any case, European population figures appear derisory in relation to the billion and a half Chinese and the nearly-billion and a half Indians predicted in the 21st century – you could almost say guaranteed – barring natural disaster or extermination by war.

What difference does 10 million more or less in population make to each of us in the future? What repercussions will there be on the daily lives of the next two generations? Just the same, when you add up all the human losses incurred by our neighbours and allies, five million Europeans absent from roll-call in the next century will be very worrying for the future of the Community.

In fact, in quantitative terms we are bound to be placed lower down on the lists of the world's most heavily populated countries. Italy (at present 14th), the United Kingdom (at present 16th) and France (at present 17th) will in 2020 find themselves in 26th, 27th and 28th place respectively.

As for West Germany, she will quite simply have disappeared from the list![3]

Countries full of little old people

The danger, however, lies not so much in the overall drop

3. See in Appendix II the tables of 'The 30 most heavily populated countries in the world' estimation for 1985 and projection for 2020.

in the number of citizens as in the distribution of the generations. When age pyramids begin to look more like Christmas trees than Egyptian tombs, the social balance is running into grave danger, because there are two ways of being included in the ranks of the living: by being born, or by not dying.

Since the beginning of the century, we have concentrated our efforts on favouring the second hypothesis: expectation of life has increased considerably in the developed countries. A male child born today can expect to live seventy-two years on average, while girls have every chance of celebrating their eightieth birthdays, and one-tenth of them will see their ninetieth spring.

The result is that the populations of Western countries increase by a minute amount each year thanks mainly to the immigrants – although they have slowed down considerably partly due to unemployment – but also to the fact that old people are living longer.

The people of all nations in the world suffer from rheumatism and get grey-haired. The industrial countries are naturally the ones who are most affected because they are the ones who have made the most spectacular progress in medicine and prevention of disease. The country that is ageing the most rapidly is Japan. The over sixty-fives represented 8.9% of the population in 1980 – by the end of the century they will be nearly 15%. In 2020, one-fifth of all the large industrial countries will be older than sixty-five.

One person in five with his life already behind him, one in five who would rather live on his memories than make new plans, one in five more or less dependent on the rest of the nation to subsidize him, look after him and help to relieve his loneliness and boredom. It's a lot – it's out of all proportion.

When is this likely to come about? From 2020 onwards, when I shall certainly be dead. Even by doing regular exercises, giving up alcohol – or very nearly – and not smoking more than five cigarettes a day, I shan't be alive after 2020. I'm saying this to make you realize that I'm not worried about *my* retirement – I'm not making a plea for myself, but for my grandchildren. For my great-grandchildren as well, because more and more of us will get to know our great-grandchildren before we make way for them.

In fact, I'm speaking to their parents. A society like the one described in all the current forecasts scares me. I don't want you and your children to live in a cramped, elderly community governed by a gerontocracy which is more preoccupied with hanging on to the advantages it has acquired than in having new ideas and investing in new enterprises.

Young adults must be wondering about the society in which their only child, or two little darlings, will be living. It isn't at all tempting. A country is like a family: its atmosphere is better if the generations live side by side in balanced harmony. Too many children and the present looks bad as it is overshadowed by preparations for the future. Too many old people and the present looks bad as it is overshadowed by reference to the past.

How unfair!

If the children of the baby boom who are now old enough to be parents in their turn don't succeed in reversing the sharp decline in the birthrate, they will have to face up to the harsh reality of a world consisting of senior citizens when they themselves reach retirement. The democracies will ossify when the main part of their inheritance is in the hands of conservatives who are more concerned with saving their capital then investing it, which is normal at that age!

The problem for those who are trying to get people to listen to these sorts of warnings is that in demography there is a gap of twenty years between the time when people take individual decisions and the time when their consequences make themselves felt by the community.

The threat of non-payment of pensions scares fifty-year olds in the 1980s, even though they really have nothing to reproach themselves for when it comes to the birthrate.

By their youthful fertility they have maintained a respectable birthrate in the developed countries. And now they're being told that in fifteen years' time, because of a decline in the working population due to a shortage of young people coming into the job market, they can't necessarily be assured of a pension equivalent to that at present drawn by those lucky devils who have already left to dig their allotments! How unfair!

First of all, let them reassure themselves. Unpaid pensions will be a worry for their children, not for themselves. Having horrified middle-aged workers by announcing there wouldn't be enough cash in the bank to pay for their old age, the experts did their sums again and realized that it's not until about 2003 that the working population will begin to decline.

Because of this, towards 2005 the retirement systems might, due to reallocation, begin to have difficulty in preserving their financial equilibrium. Phew! There's some justice after all!

But hang on a moment – a quick calculation: in 2005 the celebrated generation of women born in 1930 – the one I belong to, which in the whole history of France produced the largest number of live children – will be seventy-five years old. We shan't all be dead, not by a long way, and we're the ones who will see our pensions being gradually cut back due to lack of funds. No, there's no justice!

There certainly are no policies or long-term guarantees covering the birthrate. The generations who have the children are not necessarily the ones who profit from the economic benefits and growth in population. In the same way, the non-prolific generations live more comfortably in the short term, without worrying about the long-term effect of the decreased birthrate.

Tomorrow is another century, 'après nous le déluge!'

The German flame is burning lower and lower

West Germany is a typical example of this short-sighted

behaviour. She is the holder of two absolute records, historic and worldwide, where the birthrate is concerned:

- the fertility rate for West Germany is the lowest in the world: 1.27 children per woman;
- West Germany has the highest percentage of childless couples in the world.

A few years ago, Karl Carstens, then President of West Germany, when interviewed on the television by a French journalist on the danger of a revival of German nationalism, replied calmly: 'Europeans need have no fear of Pan-Germanism. In future the German flame will burn lower and lower before going out completely two centuries from now . . .' It's difficult to imagine a foreign leader using the decline in population as an argument to appease his suspicious neighbours!

Certain demographers have well and truly calculated that if they don't increase their birthrate in the next few years, the Germans such as they are, will disappear in about 200 years. If the present tendency continues, the population of West Germany, currently estimated to be 56 million inhabitants plus five million foreigners, will only be 20 million by 2078. A century later, there won't be a single West German left on the earth.

When you consider how the French despair about their rate of 1.8, you would imagine the West Germans, with a rate of 1.2, being assailed from all sides by extensive media campaigns begging them not to commit collective suicide by gradual extinction! Not a bit of it. For historical as well as political and sociological reasons, Germany just doesn't want to discuss anything to do with babies. She accepts the fact that her population is decreasing all the time.

Michel Meyer, a television correspondent in Bonn and author of several books on Germany, is one of the best informed Frenchmen on this country's mentality, and has several explanations for this phenomenon. Some are typically German, others confirm the conclusions arrived at by sociologists in all countries to explain the current birthrate crisis.

Specifically German reasons

A typically German Wagneresque sort of philosophy of hopeless nihilism prevails amongst students. Because it cultivates the threat of the nuclear holocaust and the inevitable destruction of the environment, it discourages young people from having children. Equally, it conjures up the threat of an enormous population explosion in the Third World which will unleash itself on the whole of Europe. What's the point of having children when there are too many already in the world?

The campaigns by the Greens, denouncing the destruction of the German forests and the dangers of radioactivity undoubtedly discourage young couples from having babies. The fact that West Germany is short of space and greenery only adds weight to their arguments. Losing the eastern part of the country has cut her off from her large forests and open spaces. All she has left are the most densely populated areas, containing towns and factories, which may be beneficial from the economic point of view, but hardly provide a suitable environment for bringing up children.

At 248 inhabitants to the square kilometer, the German density is two and a half times that of France. With the result that, in spite of their plunging birthrate, the Germans still find themselves too numerous for their overcrowded suburbs. A German woman with four children said to me:

'At home, I'm considered rather a freak with my gang. Our towns and suburbs simply aren't made to welcome children – we don't set aside enough play areas where they can run and let off steam, just one squeaking little swing beside the car park – and they're not even allowed to use that between one and three in case they disturb the pensioners while they take their siestas.

Most German women find children a nuisance; they're noisy and make a mess of everything. In the block of flats where I lived before moving into a house, my children weren't allowed to use the stairs on their own in case they spoilt the paintwork by running their hands up and down the walls. The concierge reported me to the police because one of my sons was playing ball in the courtyard, and she was afraid he might break a window pane. Parents are continually having cases brought against them because of their children. We had to take out a special insurance.

You should see people's agonised expressions when they see a child riding a bicycle – they're always terrified that he might scratch the paintwork of their precious cars!

Do you realise that in our country we don't take our children to public places if we want to avoid trouble and unpleasant remarks. You French are different – you take your children everywhere with you, while we leave ours at home.'

Knowing both countries very well, she assured me that this sort of anti-child 'racism' was typically German, but I'm not as convinced of this as she was. There's not much to choose between either country when it comes to this sort of thing!

Another specific cause of the falling birthrate is Germany's lack of a national identity. Split up because of its past, torn by being divided into two sister countries at loggerheads with one another, and cut off from its national culture since 1945, Germany, unable to live in the shadow of her past, has not yet regained her future direction.

Michel Meyer explains it in this way:

'A nation never grinds to a halt all by itself. A society whose fertility has lost its drive, whose creativity is disintegrating and whose aspirations have petrified, is sick. Not even the greatest economic achievements can change this. . . . Being German is not a source of pride, either now or in the future.'

Do the roots of a family, a region, a religion or a nation

really play a part in the child-wish? That's what German demographers think anyway when they tear their hair out, faced with all those empty cradles.

The sociological and economic consequences of the falling birthrate in West Germany are beginning to make themselves felt. They are interesting to note because *Germany is the first Western country whose birthrate has decreased in real terms*, in absolute figures over the last ten years, emigrants and foreigners included.

The first obvious victim is State education. Classes are closed at the beginning of each school year. Forty thousand infant teachers are already out of work, and 150,000 other teachers are expected to be without a job in 1990.

The second institution to be threatened is national defence. Classes of eighteen-year old boys, who are coming up to military service, are beginning to get too small. Some military experts think that it will soon be necessary to reduce the German Army's strength to 50,000 men. The Bundeswehr has even considered raising a 'foreign legion' from amongst the sons of foreign workers, or to appeal to women to make up for the lack of recruits.

Obviously, because of an ageing population, social benefits for the elderly will have to be reconsidered, and German workers will find this hard to swallow as it represents political and social 'treason'.

Finally, industry is going through a crisis in all sections which produce consumer goods for the very young. Manufacturers of ice creams and children's clothes are badly affected.

West German politicians are beginning to concern themselves with this situation, although up until now they have refused to broach these subjects for fear of upsetting public opinion, which is totally opposed to any population expansion. However, they are at a loss as to how to approach it.

At the mention of the word 'birthrate', the spectre of Nazism is immediately invoked in the subconscious. Young people 'don't know Hitler any more', but they still quote from speeches of the Third Reich, with their exhortations to German women to give birth to warriors, and their campaigns glorifying pure Aryan babies with blond hair and blue eyes. National Socialism's evil spells haven't been finally exorcised – any discussion that smacks remotely of the birthrate is in danger of being dubbed 'neo-Fascist'.

East German policy

The leaders of East Germany haven't come up against the same ideological barriers. Devoid of complexes towards their Nazi past (doesn't it go without saying that you are anti-Fascist if you're a member of the Communist bloc?), East German leaders didn't even hesitate before 'telling people what to do in bed'. In the seventies, the situation appeared disastrous from a demographic point of view. The heavy losses brought about by three and a half million defectors emigrating to the West between 1948 and 1961, together with a birthrate as low as West Germany's, led to East Germany taking a whole series of measures to encourage the birthrate while at the same time maintaining the female workforce, which was vital to the economic plan.

This effort was unique in Europe because it contained measures which anticipated in particular:

- A substantial increase in maternity allowances.
- One year's maternity leave after the first child.
- An extra year after the second child.
- A reduction in working hours and extra time off for mothers with several children.
- A free loan of 10,000 Deutschmarks for young married couples under twenty-six years old, to be paid back over eight years (the amount to be paid back being decreased by 1,000 marks on the birth of the first child, 1,500 marks on that of the second and 2,500 marks on that of the third).
- Grants for schoolchildren and students from large families.
- Personal tax allowances, etc.

A family of three children was given as the norm for purposes of comparison. The objective was to encourage women to be 'producers', of goods as well as children, both functions being essential to the future of the socialist State.

This policy had an almost immediate effect: marriage and the birthrate went shooting up in East Germany. Experts from all over the world began quoting East Germany's example when they wanted to prove that a proper birthrate policy could bear fruit. Nevertheless, since the years 1981–2, a new shrinkage has taken place. In the spring of 1986, new measures were due to be taken once again to reinforce the 'privileges' of families with three children or more.

This all seems to demonstrate that, having thought they were going to be able to offload part of their domestic duties, East German women suddenly discovered there was a wide gap between theory and reality. In 70% of households there is no equality when it comes to household tasks, even though husband and wife both work. The mother continues to pack two days into one.

In other words, whether they live in the East or the West, with or without interference from the State, it seems that German women no longer want large families because they haven't succeeded in finding a satisfactory way of reconciling their domestic and working lives.

We're seeing here once again all the recurrent themes which run through every aspect of women's responsibilities: their transformation, their liberation, their changing role within marriage, their refusal to sacrifice their jobs to motherhood, their abdication from their traditional function, their search for a new balance in modern society. . . . No-one actually dares use the word 'lack': socialists and liberals have once and for all admitted the right of women to be full citizens. However, in many of the analyses which I've read on the German situation, one can detect a sort of feeling of regret, a nostalgia for the 'three K's'[4], going back

4. '*Kirchen, Kinder, Küchen*': The Church, Children and Cooking, the three pillars of the feminine condition in Germany since the beginning of the century.

to the time when German women were the best housewives in Europe!

Therefore, it's the same in all the rich countries: women have changed, and so has the whole domestic routine of which they were the central pivot.

Germany is unarguably the most extreme example of these domestic transformations. They rarely do things by halves in that country, which is why they have repressed their child-wish even more systematically. Disliking compromise in any form, could they be just a little too inflexible to think up new ways of organizing their domestic lives to allow for the expectations of modern women?

V

Child-Wish And Birth Control

A week late – panic. Those who were 'overdue' used to arrive on Monday mornings looking haggard, with dark rings under their eyes. All night they had been trying to work out when they should have had their period. There was no doubt, they were a week late. Why was it always at the weekend that you were certain you were overdue? There wasn't time on the other days, and anyway weeks are rounded off on Sunday and begin again on Monday. Until Sunday came you allowed yourself a 'natural' margin for error. After that you really started to worry.

At the factory or the office, between neighbours or colleagues, the word very soon got around. 'Don't worry, it must be the heat (or the cold, depending on the time of year). You're too tired – it'll come back . . .' Others who were more realistic got straight down to offering practical advice: 'My sister-in-law knows a chemist who gave her a fantastic purge which got her going'.

No-one really believed in these old wives' remedies, but they were all prepared to try anything that might bring on their periods and soothe their anxiety.

It's true that two times out of three *it* came back – not all ovaries work like clockwork. Often, however, even though you made yourself lift heavy objects, take boiling hot baths and try lots of injections to make your muscles contract, nothing did any good and you had to face up to 'biological' reality: you had 'fallen' pregnant. A pregnancy test only confirmed your worst fears.

The horror of a back-street abortion

Then, the privileged were faced with two agonizing alternatives: either to have another baby or to risk the horror of a back-street abortion. Women in low social brackets had no choice but to resign themselves unwillingly to often repeated pregnancies, as abortions were very expensive – not far off £2,000 to £3,000 in today's money.

Even if you could find the money, stories of perforated wombs, lethal injections or emergency admissions to hospital where doctors curetted you without an anaesthetic to teach you not to play forbidden games, hardly encouraged you to trust yourself to some old crone in a back street. Except in cases of insoluble personal dramas, unknown fathers, doubtful paternities, rape, incest or an already over-sized family, you weren't prepared to risk your fertility, your health or your life. I've always admired women who've had the courage to have abortions in such conditions of physical danger and emotional distress. I never have myself.

Gradually, being overdue changed into being pregnant. You became resigned to the idea that you were expecting a baby. With a bit of luck, your family and friends gave you some encouragement. The husband and father – nine out of ten of us were married before twenty-five – feeling at least half responsible for this 'mistake' also accepted his responsibilities. It wasn't joy, but it was life.

A few months later, joy and life were reconciled: you had a baby.

Even when not necessarily planned, I have always been amazed by how great an event the arrival of a newborn baby was in my life. The day before, all you can think about is giving birth, about 'setting down' the incredible burden which has taken possession of your intimate 'territory'. A little while later, having spent a few not very pleasant hours – whatever magazines for young parents may say[1] – this little mite arrives, exists, and makes his

1. Rhapsodizing about the fabulous emotions aroused during the miraculous experience of childbirth has always left me a bit sceptical. Having a baby, especially with the help of modern methods, is neither

mark as a personality. In a few seconds, as soon as they show him to you, all crumpled, not quite recovered from his long stay inside you, you forget that yesterday there was a world in which he wasn't an essential part of your life.

Two children instead of one don't cause too much havoc, but three instead of two make life more complicated and budgets tighter. Women gave up their careers so they could devote themselves to bringing up their 'little' families. They missed their work, their salaries, their independence and their personal lives, but most women were in the same boat. They felt a bit frustrated, but their husbands seemed satisfied with their decision. . . .

When sex and procreation went hand-in-hand

From then on you had to take every precaution not to spend your whole life either expecting or nursing. The husband had to 'be careful', and put up with our precautions. We were quite determined sex wouldn't play any more tricks on us! We lived with a calendar in our hands. To avoid running risks, we ended up cutting down more and more on the days when we said 'yes'. We were more hesitant than abandoned when the light went out, and began to understand how our mothers had become frigid. When sex and procreation went hand in hand, one had to be firmly suppressed to control the other.

Birth control isn't a modern invention. Intelligent women have always managed to keep the upper hand over their fertility. What is new, vital and revolutionary since the arrival of the pill and the coil is the reliability of these methods. Since the 18th century, middle-class women have by one means or another managed to limit their children to a maximum of two or three. English and French women in particular had whole arsenals of elixirs and different

the damnable, unbearable suffering it used to be, nor a fun outing. It's hard physical labour which doesn't encourage thoughts of poetry or metaphysics while it's going on. Like all performances, it's only when you see the result that you realize what you've been through.

gadgets at their disposal to bar the way of the sperm. With a bit of luck, a bad infection left you sterile. Otherwise, abstinence was strongly advocated, and considered rather '*distinguée*' for those unfortunate women who got pregnant as soon as anyone looked at them.

Women were in fact practising demography without realizing it. By having fewer children, they were compensating for the progress in perinatal and infant medicine. The fewer infant deaths there are, the fewer babies you need to end up with a reasonable sized family once your child-bearing days are over. Two hundred years ago, simply to replace the generations women needed to have eight pregnancies or more to make up for the high infant mortality of that period, as well as widowhood and premature sterility amongst women like themselves. In our day, we have the incredible good fortune of seeing 995 out of 1,000 of our children grow up.

Therefore, it's only to be expected that large families should have disappeared – they are no longer needed to ensure the survival of the species. The few eccentrics who indulge themselves with hordes of children in the same way as other people collect vintage cars are giving way to an outdated passion which can no longer be justified as vital for our survival.

From now on, two or three children are enough to replace the generations. It's the increasing number of couples who only have one child that is a danger to the birthrate. All in all, now that there is no longer an element of chance, having children has ceased to seem necessary.

Why has this become such a difficult decision to make? Having lived through both periods, 'before' and 'after' birth control, which is scientific rather than makeshift, I am rather astonished that women should have reacted in such a restrained manner. The new power they are holding in their hands certainly hasn't gone to their heads – or very little has. They still want to live with men, and they haven't entirely given up having children. After the revolution we have just experienced, which is still going on in its physical form, a lower birthrate was the least we could expect in the way of a reaction.

The revolution in contraception

Over the last twenty years, we women have experienced a fundamental physiological transformation in our circumstances: the scientific control by women of their own fertility.[2] The pill is by no means the perfect solution for everyone, but it does mark an important stage in relationships between men and women and between parents and children, because above all it has radically changed women's attitude towards their own motherhood.

It's true that not all women are well informed about different contraception techniques. Even those who are don't always scrupulously follow the instructions given for their use. In barely twenty years you can hardly expect to alter attitudes, permit what had been forbidden, avoid subconscious fears, distrust of drugs and moral reservations to any great extent. The very young don't dare ask for advice and those a little older fluctuate between personal logic and their subconscious desire for a child. Lots of pills that should have been taken get 'forgotten'. Far too many abortions still take place which could have been avoided. Women aren't robots, for heaven's sake! They all have their own inconsistencies, emotions, worries and desires. Personally, I think that if anything they have absorbed this new improvement in their circumstances with unforeseeable speed.

Historically, the legalization of abortion[3] will only appear as an episode in this transformation. It was needed to stop the carnage of back-street abortions, to give women control over their own fertility and to avoid unbearable

2. If scientific birth control had been for men, would there be more or less children today? That's an interesting question! In fact, no pill for men is predicted for the future. The only method practised for men is sterilization which has the drawback of being irreversible.

3. Great Britain was the first country to legalize abortion in 1967. Holland has shown leniency towards abortion on demand since 1970, but this was an 'illegal' leniency. The law authorizing it in France was only passed in 1984!

personal crises of which unwanted babies often became innocent victims.

For the future: contragestion

We should also consider the next step in scientific birth control – the 'morning after' method – as being even more revolutionary, because it will be easier to use and simpler to fit into everyday life. Contragestion will therefore replace contraception.[4]

For several years now research has been going on to produce substances capable of blocking progesterone, the hormone which is essential for all gestation as it permits incubation of the fertilised egg. In France, an anti-progesterone substance, RU 486, has been experimented with in a dozen or so hospitals. It's already known that it brings on a sort of 'miscarriage' in most of the women taking part in the clinical trials without any side effects or risk of infection. Therefore, the idea is to use it as a 'contragestive' at the end of a cycle to bring on the periods of those who have had sexual relations during the whole of the previous month without using any contraceptives at all.

One can easily see the advantages of this method over the pill, the main one being that it would suit all women who don't have a regular sex life, whether they are adolescents, single women, divorcees or women living alone. They wouldn't need to block their cycle for a whole year to be ensured of protection if they should start an affair.

Dr Serfati, of the Hopital St Louis, Paris, estimates that 133 of the 600 or 700 terminations carried out each year in his hospital could have been avoided if women, knowing they had had intercourse during the period of ovulation, had been able to avail themselves of 'morning after' contraception.

4. Contraception = various methods employed to render a man or woman infertile. Contragestion = various methods employed to prevent gestation in a woman.

Why go into such detail on birth control in a book devoted to children? Because I'm convinced that 'voluntary' motherhood, which is the result of a responsible decision and has been planned practically down to the exact month, will be the rule from now on. Haven't we already heard of certain maternity hospitals planning to charge different fees according to the months of the year to ease their seasonal difficulties? Just as with tourism and travel, there will be months when you will be able to have babies more cheaply if you do it 'off season'. A room in a private maternity hospital would be twice as cheap in October, November or January as in May or June, which is the high season for babies as everyone wants to have them before the summer so that they can tack their annual paid holiday on to their maternity leave.

Unlike oysters, the baby market is slack during the months with an 'R'!

There will always be unplanned babies, but they will be the exception. In ten years, the proportion of unwanted pregnancies has already decreased by a half, going down from 15% to 9% of all births. From now on we won't be able to count on the 'accidents' to push up the birthrate.

How can we fail to rejoice at the fact that human beings have conquered their own destiny? The more we can subdue 'the beast' in us, the more exciting life becomes – but exciting doesn't mean simple. It's better to complicate your life by making your own choices than to put up with events over which you feel you have no control.

As a woman, I've always found it marvellous to give life deliberately, having made up my mind to do so.

Being active, not passive

Before accusing young women who have neither the desire nor the need to have children of being selfish, we should be quite sure we understand the difficulty of making this vital decision to bring a child into the world, particularly when knowing that for twenty years one will have to be completely responsible for him or her. This is a decision which will be 'active', not 'passive' from now on.

When I spoke highly of the advantages of wanted children to a psychologist with two children of her own, she had this reaction:

'I've often thought to myself how lucky I was to have a family. When I got married in the early sixties, neither the pill nor other contraceptive methods were widely available. I didn't really feel strongly one way or the other about being a mother. My husband was studying and I was teaching – we were very young, and there was no "sensible" reason why we should have children.

As newly-weds, we thought we were being careful, but we certainly weren't careful enough as I had my two children in three years. Not entirely by chance – being a psychologist I don't believe in chance in these sorts of circumstances – but rather by casualness. I'm sure my subconscious allowed my desire for children to have its way.

I'm very grateful for this now because I adored being a mother, and I can't imagine what my life would have been like without children. However, I've often wondered whether I would have had the courage to stop taking the pill deliberately, knowing that I would get pregnant within a few weeks. In fact, I've got proof of this: after the second child was born I started using a reliable contraceptive and I've never had a third child. I often thought about it, but there were always more reasons for giving up the idea than for going through with it.

I admire young women of today who go into motherhood with their eyes wide open.'

It's true that it takes courage to bring children into the world, the sort of courage that's always needed to make difficult decisions which have a heavy bearing on the future – they have to be made without all the facts at your finger tips to make you certain that your decision was well-founded.

How much do we really know of what's in store for us when we start a baby? In nine months' time will we produce either a source of happiness or grounds for anxiety and sadness? Do we really feel adult enough to have a baby in our turn? Will the couple formed by us and the future father at the moment of the baby's conception be capable of changing harmoniously into a family? In a year's time will we have discovered how to ensure the child's welfare if we carry on working? In five years will we still be living with the father? In ten years, will our standard of living have gone down as a result of economic difficulties, or will we be as well or better off than we are today? In twenty years will the whole planet have been devastated by nuclear war?

Frankly, such a list shouldn't be published in a book like this. It might put off would-be mothers for ever!

The child-wish won't go away

What amazes me is that in spite of all the disasters that threaten us, all the changes that confront us, all the individual risks we have to take, the practical difficulties that have to be solved to reconcile domestic and professional life – in spite of unemployment, the economic crisis, general and individual insecurity, widespread divorce, decline in marriage, the indifference displayed by most Western societies to young children and their mothers, the increase in individualism, the change in family customs – in spite of all these, the child-wish won't go away.

Could it be because it's so firmly rooted in human nature! Particularly female human nature.

Don't ask me for any metaphysical explanations to justify my theory – I haven't got any. I think it's enough to remember my own experiences and to listen to other women expressing themselves in similar ways. I'm a great believer in the fact that the question of whether or not to have children isn't a strictly rational one. There are subconscious forces lying in wait in our minds to urge us to give life in the same way as our parents gave it to us. These forces come from far away – they ignore our insignificant, humdrum personal arguments, our payslips and our rents and tell us that we are links in a chain which we mustn't break. Some women, and I'm among them, are more sensitive to this irrational demand. Others prove to be less instinctive and are more easily held back by prevailing circumstances – they are more resistant to the child-wish.

These restraints are multiplying – they are getting stronger all the time in modern life. They are more and more successful in putting off the first pregnancy, and in holding up the following ones. Nevertheless, the desire is still there, as strong as ever, even though it's not given in to as often as it would like.

By preventing unwanted pregnancies, contraception makes women responsible for their descendants. The situation is complicated: when you're at the age when you can have children easily you don't always want them; on the other hand, when you really want them you haven't always got time to have enough.

The imaginary last child

I've always felt certain that most women feel a 'lack' concerning the number of children they've bought up. I've met hundreds who, as I do, often feel they would have liked one more. They admit secretly that they regret not having had this imaginary last child.

No national poll has ever studied this particular subject. To have a clear mind, therefore, I undertook a mini-poll, which wasn't at all representative, but was nevertheless quite significant.

In Paris there's a club for women executives, the Club 'L', whose members meet once a month to pool their professional experiences and exchange addresses and points of view. All those who belong hold responsible positions in various sectors of the economy. They have 'made a career for themselves' in the traditionally male sense of the word. The Club 'L' has about 200 members.

During our meetings I've frequently noticed that domestic matters come up very often in our conversations. One of us even said:

> 'It's incredible what good housewives we are! One way or the other, we nearly always end up talking about our kids or our husbands during an evening. I'm sure that our male counterparts are much more reticent about their personal lives!'

These women's attitudes to motherhood interested me in that they were all typical of the 'successful' woman, and were valid examples of young women of today. Therefore I asked them if they would reply to a questionnaire on their desire for children. To get the most genuine results possible they answered anonymously, without any preceeding explanation by me.

Mini-poll of career women

The questions were as follows:
Are you single, married, divorced, widowed?
Number of children?
Age of children?
Do you consider you have had not enough, enough, or too many children?

All of them answered willingly; they all felt directly concerned with this question of the place taken up by children in their lives. The discussions after I had collected up their papers proved to me that they had already thought about this in their heart of hearts.

It was possible to glean three pieces of information from the results:

1. Career women's family situations are very similar to those of the average woman

70% are married, 10% divorced, 5% widows and 15%

single. The low divorce rate is rather surprising, especially for women graduates (but among those who declared themselves 'married', there must have been a certain number of 'remarrieds').

2. Their professional lives and their success hadn't stopped them from having children

60% had two children or more (two children: 28%, three children: 23%, four children or more: 9%). One third of mothers with three children or more: this is a high figure which doesn't necessarily correspond with the generally accepted idea of 'career women'.

Only 19% were mothers of only children, and 21% had no children at all. Had they refused to have children in order to devote more time to their careers, or had they devoted the major part of their lives to being successful because they weren't mothers? We get some sort of a reply thanks to the question on satisfaction. Half of them regretted not being mothers and the others didn't reply to the question. Only one, an airline pilot, said she was happy not to have any children:

> 'I didn't have any children because I didn't want to. I didn't put my career first, I just didn't feel dedicated by nature to having children. If I'd been a secretary I wouldn't have had any either. I think that women who have lots of children are terribly bored. I have so many interests that I don't need a child to keep me busy. You can't explain why you don't want children – or why you want a lot for that matter.'

These women who choose not to have children are few and far between. Let's hope there aren't more of them in the year 2000!

3. Career women don't regret the children they've had. Two out of three would have liked more

Consider they haven't had enough children	60%
Consider they have had enough children	34%
Consider they have had too many children	1%
Don't reply	6%

Only the women with four or more children consider they've had too many. Of those with three or less, a clear majority wish they hadn't stopped there. The fact that most women regret they didn't have more children is to be expected in childless women, makes sense in those with only children, nine out of ten of whom feel restricted as mothers, is slightly more surprising in mothers of two children, but it's astonishing in mothers of three children.

It makes you wonder whether children aren't like money – the more you have the more you want.

Those holding conservative, traditional views might conclude from this that career women keep such strict control over the number of their children that they suppress their maternal yearnings even if later on they regret having 'sacrificed' their family to their personal ambition. What wicked, selfish women to offer themselves the luxury of a mind as well as a womb! QED: if more of them gave up their professional ambitions, the birthrate would rise.

This is a classic argument, but it's meaningless. For a long time now sociologists have demonstrated that fertility figures are far from being in inverse proportion to those for women who work. Holland is the best known example, where the percentage of women who work is low, but the birthrate is nevertheless mediocre.

Mini-poll of women at home

To be quite clear in my mind, having completed my mini-poll of career women, I submitted the same questionnaire to a club for 'women at home'. I imagined that they would have more children and less regrets than their 'busy' sisters. I was shattered by the similarity in situations and attitudes.

The only noticeable difference was that the group consisted of less single women, a few more married women and widows than that of the career women, and above all no divorcees (it was more traditionalist in the way it recruited its members). Once again taking the same precautions over its use, and emphasizing that this wasn't research on a national scale, I compared the results of the two groups and extracted two pieces of information:

1. Women who don't go out to work don't have many more children than the others

A few less families with only children, a few more large families but, as in the case of the career women, the balance centred around two children. Curiously enough, the career women had more families with three children, but that could be due to an anomaly having crept into my not very strict sampling!

2. There are as many of them as there are of career women who think they 'could have done better'

	Women at home	Career women
Consider they haven't had enough children	62%	60%
Consider they have had enough children	35%	34%
Consider they've had too many children	0%	1%
Don't reply	3%	6%

When comparing these two columns of figures, the conclusion is significant: two-thirds of women questioned expressed a lingering feeling that they hadn't 'had enough'. Aware of the risks and responsibilities another child would entail, and employing common sense and effective birth control, they had given up the idea of having a baby either as a love-child, afterthought, present or surprise. If it had arrived by chance they would have welcomed it with open arms, but they couldn't make up their minds to send it an invitation.

Another probable reason was that it takes two to invite one more to join the feast, and men aren't always very enthusiastic when it comes to laying an extra place for the family supper.

VI

Men Are More Husbands Than Fathers

'In the old days, a blacksmith only had one ambition: to turn his son into a blacksmith like himself – to teach him the trade and, before he died, to see his son take over the family forge and enlarge it. When you're a wage earner as I am, you can't hand on a skill which you know will probably be obsolete by the time your sons grow up, but you can hand on a taste for learning; you can teach him to learn, or just pass on to him a desire for knowledge. Unfortunately, that takes a lot of time. If a father has three children, and you think he should devote at least one hour a day to each child, how can he possibly give up three hours a day to their upbringing?'

Luke is thirty-two, and father of two – he's a supervisor in a multinational company and so far the idea hasn't crossed his mind that he might have a third child one day. Nevertheless, fatherhood agrees with him. Having listened to him for three hours taking part in a group discussion on 'Men and the desire for children', I was touched by his warmth and gentleness and by his obvious involvement when talking about his family. He loves his wife, is quite devoted to his two kids (especially the little one who is only a few months old) and shows no sign at all either that his marriage is going through a bad patch or that he's bored by his family. Luke is as happy as Larry, and quite content to give up a lot of time to his family to help out his wife who works as well. Unless in a few years' time she manages to persuade him that they really ought to have a third child, he will be quite happy to rest on his laurels.

Different categories of fathers

When preparing this book, I was amazed at how little information and research had been done on the part played by men in the birthrate question. You always talk about the number of 'children per woman', never 'per man'. You question mothers about their various attitudes to having children, but you very rarely question fathers. In demography, men still have a very conservative role – they are 'the head of the family' and are characterized by their professions. Their fertility figures are totally ignored. Nothing has been done in this area to find out whether there are for example:

Conscious fathers: they know what they're doing, and take their full share of responsibility for having children.

Cheated fathers: they are faced with a *fait accompli* without having even been asked whether they want to have a family or not.

Swamped fathers: they happen to love a prolific woman who is only happy if she's living in a house full of bunkbeds and yelling children.

Authoratitive fathers: they have a genuine desire for children and expect their wives to provide them with the required number.

Half-hearted fathers: they deny their wives' desire for children because they themselves have no wish to take on the responsibility of a large family.

Frustrated fathers: they would like to surround themselves with little fair-haired children, but come up against a blank wall where their other halves – the ones who do the carrying – are concerned.

Prolific fathers: they have one or more children by every woman who comes into their lives. Some have a particular bent for starting their paternal career young and carrying it on till late in life – they often have young children and grandchildren all at once, male fertility having no age limit!

Sterile fathers: in spite of themselves, they never have any 'biological' children because they act as father to those of the woman they've married. You find more and more of them amongst the 'bachelor' companions of divorced women who are older than they are.

Unmarried fathers: they would like to rent a womb to carry their child so as to avoid having to share it later on with a woman.

There is evidence that all these fathers exist; however, they hardly ever express their opinions because no-one ever questions them. National newspapers are more interested in frozen sperm than fathers. The female press advises its readers on the emergence of professional 'father-hens'. The male press hardly ever presents fathers as parents or educators. They're only interested in captains of industry or leading personalities in sport, culture or sex as worthy examples.

Another characteristic of present research is endless discussion on fathers by psychoanalysts, by women and, above all, by women psychoanalysts to find out how to include the father in the discussions on mothers and children, and to try and decide what role to give this character whose function is no longer clearly defined now that the day of the patriarch is over, and women have seized the power to be mothers by desire and not by submission to the father.

In search of experienced fathers

I wasn't looking for theories. I needed facts, real fathers talking about their experiences, describing their hopes and disappointments and thinking about their role as 'new fathers'.

Thanks to SYNESIS, a market research company

which specializes in socio-psychological studies, I had the opportunity of meeting some, or rather, of listening to them. The group met in one of the rooms at the institute under the direction of two specialists – a psychologist and a market researcher. I followed the discussions on a video screen in a nearby room.

There were eight men between the ages of twenty-four and forty. The youngest was expecting a baby in two months, the 'veteran' had three children, all at school. Six were married and two 'lived with' the mothers of their children. They spoke quite frankly and openly – they had never met before, and they knew that nothing they said could ever be linked with them. Luke was on this panel.

Some significant ideas emerged from what they said – and from what they didn't say.

About the child-wish

What they said:

> 'Children aren't a tie for those who have them, only for those who are thinking of having them.'

> 'It's at the planning stage that you count up all the negative factors that an extra child represents. Once he's there it's quite different.'

What about having a child? Yes, why not, but not straight away. They all admit it's the wife's idea. She asks the question and she wants an answer, but she doesn't want to force the issue. At the beginning, young wives seem to have a much more urgent desire for children than their husbands.

Young men no longer seem to feel they have any right to refuse to let a woman have a child if she wants one. Nor, incidentally, to be able to make her have one if they want one themselves. They are only too well aware of the 'cost' of motherhood to women in general, and their wives in particular. However willing or determined they may be to share in domestic duties or to help look after the children, they admit that the heaviest burden will fall on the mother.

She is the one who will have to carry the child, who will have to give birth to it and who will be mainly responsible for solving practical problems and organizing everyday routine – in the end, she will be the one who has to re-think her professional status, her way of living, her timetable, her career and her whole future.

They prove to be very honest on this point. Although they share in the household duties and really help to care for the baby in the early days, and to look after him through the various stages till he's older, they only see themselves as assistants. They realize that the chief responsibility rests on the wife's shoulders.

In most cases they have agreed to have a child 'to make her happy', having first of all tried to put the idea off for as long as possible. One should have a bit of fun out of life before giving up one's freedom!

This is shown up in all research: young couples are putting off the first baby longer and longer. In the sixties, a large proportion of couples had their first babies between the eighth and sixteenth month of marriage, which meant that these children were conceived very early on in the marriage. In 1980 the first birth occurred more and more frequently between eighteen months and three years of marriage.

Sociologists nearly always attribute this delay to the young wives, who want to take advantage of a few extra years' freedom to consolidate their careers before taking on financial responsibilities. Listening to young fathers talking, you get the impression that they are equally responsible for this postponement. They're not exactly in a hurry to give up their youthful irresponsibility!

A frequent example given by the young fathers to show how tied they had become, was the cinema. Being able to go to the cinema when you feel like it after work in the evenings is something that definitely has to be given up when a baby arrives. From now on you're condemned to baby-sitting in front of the telly. When babies need their evening bottles, you have to give up your evening drinks with friends!

Men know that fatherhood means sacrificing the carefree way they felt when they were young, which was something they hadn't taken into account when they got married. Their fathers said goodbye to bachelor life when they got married because they accepted the fact that from then on they would take complete responsibility for their wives, and would retreat into an almost exclusive relationship with them. They themselves form couples – it doesn't matter whether legally or not – with independent, liberated women who don't ask to be looked after for better or worse. Only the arrival of a child makes them realize that from now on they are responsible for another human being.

They're perfectly clear about what they're going to lose by becoming fathers, but they don't know what they're going to gain. When they were young, they never had anything to do with small children, and they've never been taught anything about fatherhood. When the time comes, their chief motive is to let their wives have their wish for a child – more to show their love for them than because they want a child themselves.

They're certainly proud that their partners should ask this of them, and that they should love them so much that they want a child like them. However, they don't really have any strong paternal feelings until they have physical contact with their very own child: 'A child is what life's about!', 'A child is our future!', 'A child is an expression of pure love!'

It seems more obvious that they should want a second child, the first one having taught them a whole new range of emotions – the delight given by loving gestures and the intensity of feeling when a child's expression shows his eagerness for his father's love.

About pregnancy and birth

What they said:

'Seeing a scan of your future baby conveys an unforgettable picture which gives you the impression that life is on the move, and that you are already in contact with the baby in his mother's womb.'

'It's the first time that we men are able to get to know our child before he's born – it's as though we're physically sharing our wife's pregnancy with her.'

'At that moment, my wife and I shared a feeling of deep emotion. Perhaps even greater than during the birth.'

The conversation about scanners was an amazing mixture of love and up-to-date technology. Nearly all of them had had the opportunity of being with their wives for this 'video'-broadcast direct from their future child. An overwhelming experience because it takes place calmly and peacefully when no-one is afraid or in pain.

At the time of the scan, the doctor generally offers to tell the parents the sex of the foetus. Half the fathers present refused to be told 'so as not to spoil the primitive surprise'. They all agreed that amongst their friends, there had been frequent errors of 'presumed sex'. They didn't want to risk having to put matters right once the baby was born. Anyway, what did it matter to them whether it was a boy or a girl! (It was doubtful whether they were being quite honest when they said they didn't mind what sex it was! They could hardly admit publicly either to a chaùvinist wish for a male heir, or to an 'Oedipus complex' for a little girl.)

When their wife is expecting a baby they talk to her at length, both about her condition and about the child to come – particularly about the former. Husbands share all their wives' primitive anxieties. They are spared none of the traditional feminine worries, from the fear of a premature baby to worrying about a Caesarean. They're only half convinced by medical progress, childbirth techniques and the care of mother and baby. They can't see any relationship between statistical risks and personal danger. Only Jeremy said that he was completely relaxed. 'She ate well and slept well, and at all her pre-natal visits the doctor said everything was fine. I couldn't see any need to worry. Besides, she adores being pregnant.' When a wife is blooming, a husband is relaxed!

On the other hand, no-one waxed lyrical about being present at the delivery. Quite the reverse, they dwelt at length on how frightened a woman must feel when she goes into the labour ward, with all its technical equipment and its medical team which is so used to the scene that its members hardly bother to reassure the mother-to-be. The word fear came up over and over again, always in connection with the wife. When I heard them speaking, I got the feeling that they were trying to get rid of their own fears – fear of suffering, fear for the mother's health and fear for the baby which they were always afraid might be 'abnormal'.

I've often wondered about fathers' 'expected' presence in the delivery room. From the women's point of view, the benefits are obvious: a familiar presence, moral support and being able to share one's emotions are reassuring and comforting.

From the men's point of view, the benefits spring less readily to mind. Are they there by solidarity rather than by personal choice? What could be more natural? We all know that most men hate anything remotely resembling a hospital. They loathe the smell of ether, white coats and sickrooms. There's no doubt they're scared to death, just as their wives are straining with all their might to give life.

Peter described how he couldn't help thinking of the stories of days gone by when the midwife used to come out of the room to ask the father: 'Things don't look too good. Who do you want to save, the mother or the child?'

Everyone had something to say about this: they thought that such a question couldn't possibly arise nowadays. How could you imagine sacrificing the life of your wife or girlfriend? Obviously, she comes first. What would be the point of a child without the mother who wanted him, carried him and brought him into the world. I suppose that never before have men realized so clearly that tiny babies belong in the first place to their mothers.

Sometimes it takes several days, weeks or even months

for an individual relationship to develop between a father and his child. Until then, men think of themselves more as companions to the baby's mother than as pater familias.

About everyday life

What they said:

> 'We often ask our wives how they feel when they're pregnant, or how our babies are when they're ill or cutting their teeth. Men are interested in all the practical aspects of children.

> 'In the sort of life we lead nothing is done to simplify the existence of young parents. Have you ever tried getting on to the underground with a pushchair? It's impossible.

> 'The other day at the office I had a long discussion with my colleagues about the different makes of disposable nappies – about which ones were leak-proof and which weren't. We had begun the conversation by discussing a telly advert. We got through our whole lunch hour without talking about cars or football!'

Not having been too keen on venturing into fatherhood before the birth, 'new fathers' undergo a radical change of behaviour, unlike their predecessors, once the baby's arrival has turned their lives upside down.

Bottles, jars of baby food, old-fashioned remedies for getting the baby to sleep at night, or calming him when he's cutting his teeth, nappy-changing and nail-cutting no longer hold any secrets from them. They've learnt how to open their arms and use both hands to see to their baby's wellbeing and their tired wife's rest.

They amaze themselves by their competence when 'bustling about' being nursemaids. Now that women have won themselves the right to be airline pilots or compete for the most sought-after university places, men have achieved the privilege of playing mother.

Certainly, not all of them intend to be full-time or even part-time 'father hens', but most of them find it quite natural to take over from their wives, especially when they work as well.

'Helping my wife'; 'Giving my wife a chance to get some rest'; 'Sharing the children's care with my wife'; with domestic tasks also, 'new fathers' relate more to their wives than their children. The 'newer' they are, the more they co-operate; the more 'pater' they are, the less they collaborate.

A study carried out by two sociologists shows that the fathers who were more hesitant about the idea of having a child in the first place often turn out to be the most conscientious 'nannies'.

'They find it perfectly natural' point out Anne-Marie Devreux and Michele Ferrand, 'that their wives should work, and sometimes find it hard to imagine any other situation. Above all, they quite systematically share parental duties and domestic work to do with the child.'

On the other hand, it has been noted that born fathers, who have always wanted to have children, have reserves about mothers who work. They clearly have a less egalitarian approach to sharing domestic duties than men who are much less positive about fatherhood.

Finally, something that, amazingly, wasn't mentioned: money. Expenses and costs played virtually no part in the discussion of negative aspects. When asked to recall practical family problems, the financial aspect came almost last, way behind the complications of daily routine, the sacrifice of leisure time and the end of a carefree, somewhat bohemian existence. 'Once you have children,' sighed John, 'You can't leave the fridge empty any more. You have to organize three meals a day, even when you're on holiday!'

Children are a hell of a tie and stop you enjoying your free time. Travelling with children? Impossible. Sport with children? Difficult, except when they're grown up. Going on holiday with children? Out of the question going without them, but how lovely to be able to dump them on the grandparents now and again and go off together on your own for a bit of peace and quiet! Weekends with children? Impossible to have a lie-in until they reach the age of reason.

Also they're not too keen on the idea of repeatedly going back to square one, with bottles at night, Sunday mornings in the park, teeth being cut, piling up the car with collapsible cot, pushchair, pottie and highchair, or having their papers, records, books and knick-knacks devastated by a vandal of eighteen months.

Fathers have absolutely no wish to postpone indefinitely the moment when the children are *finally* big enough to give them a bit of a life of their own.

About upbringing

What they said:

> 'My father was really only a "bystander" in my life. His presence was strong but, on the whole, rare. I myself want to be more than a "presence" for my children.

> 'The duty of upbringing falls more heavily than ever on the father's shoulders. Before, the extended family, including grandparents, godparents and neighbours, took over a large part of it, but now parents are almost on their own, and they have so little time to spare!'

The lack of time, already a worry at the baby stage, takes on crisis proportions for fathers when children get bigger, and preoccupation with upbringing is added on to emotional and material responsibilities.

Fathers feel they are the ones who ought to be responsible for handing on values, formation of character, intellectual curiosity and the desire for learning, understanding and knowledge. They seem to find this function an inherent part of being a father. They recall their own father on the subject – some of them because they reproach him for not having taken enough interest in them and some, on the contrary, because they are afraid they won't be able to live up to his example. All of them blame modern living for keeping them away too much from their families. What's the point of having children if you only see them for an hour each evening? In such a short time, how can you instil in them a basis for forming character and intellect?

Henry changed jobs six months ago and has thrown himself into his new work. He wants to be successful, and to fulfil his ambition to carry out a particular project. He is getting home later and later, and has no more time to help his elder daughter with her homework – she's bright but very slow. As a result her marks went down straightaway, and Henry was called in by the head, who told him he was worried and said that if the situation wasn't put right the following term, they might have to think again about whether the child would be ready for secondary school next year.

'I feel terribly guilty,' he admitted, 'But I can't jeopardize my career just to act as coach to a lazy young lady! My wife hasn't got any more time than I have. How do you think we could possibly have a third child in the circumstances?'

It seemed to me that the whole thing was easy to understand but difficult to change. The more women have involved their husbands in the upbringing and education of the children, the more they have had to share in the everyday worries that previously were the sole preserve of mothers – the more fathers find out about how much is involved in upbringing, the less they want to have children.

Fathers are nostalgic for the old days

They lovingly assume their role as 'new fathers' and appreciate the attraction of being able to develop a closer relationship with their children now that their wives no longer have exclusive responsibility for them. Nevertheless, what nostalgia they have in their voices when indulging in fantasy about 'Victorian father figures', who had their own armchair, and their place at the head of the table which they never left during the whole meal, who cast an eye over exercise books either approvingly with a smile or threateningly with a frown, and who went off on Saturday afternoons without either conscience or reproaches to watch football or go shooting, while their wives looked after the children.

'In the country where I live you can still find old-fashioned families. People who must have had money once, but have nothing left but their principles. On Sunday mornings I see them go by on their way to church. Mummy and Daddy arm-in-arm, in front or behind, and the children walking along in pairs because there are at least four of them. I'm often surprised to find I rather envy them with their principles and their polished shoes, their suits and ties and their Ford hatchbacks which are big enough for everyone including the dog. A large family is proof of the confidence a man and woman have in one another, it's an answer to important metaphysical questions, a way of combating insecurity and a sort of clan in whose shelter you can find mutual aid and identity. I'll never be the father of this sort of family, but I sometimes wish I could be!'

You might have expected Paul's reflections to provoke some irony on the part of the other participants, but not a bit of it. Most of them admitted that occasionally they too dreamt of the good old days. . . .

How can we blame them for this nostalgia? It's true that it was easier to be a father when you only had to shout to be listened to, give orders to be obeyed and sit down at table to be served. Poor modern fathers! The great craze for questioning everything and feeling guilty, which turns human relationships upside down these days slaps men full in the face.

The only glimmer of hope for the birthrate is the fact that bad consciences, guilt and doubts don't multiply arithmetically – very much the reverse: fathers of three children appear more 'laid back' than fathers of two, who are themselves less 'psyched up' than fathers of only children.

Does increasing the number of children make parents more relaxed? After giving the matter some thought, I came up with two possible explanations:

1. The mother's temperament. A woman can sometimes want a child for selfish reasons, or two children to conform, without necessarily being blessed with a highly developed maternal temperament. But if she has three, she really knows what she's taking on! She becomes completely taken up with her maternal role and shows this by her attitude to everyone, large or small – she is better than ever at easing the father's timetable as well as his guilty conscience.

2. The father's character. To put up with a large family, he needs to be optimistic and expansive by nature. Introverts, worriers, egocentrics and playboys are the ones who refuse to throw themselves into an adventure of this kind. As to the optimistic, happy-go-lucky fathers who 'collect' children, they retain the characteristics in their approach to fatherhood that pushed them into having lots of children in the first place. Therefore it's not numerous children that affect a father's good temper, but the reverse.

You're going to say that I'm biased in my analysis, and that I've got a weakness for prolific fathers. I quite agree – I admit to this tendency. These men who create new life, wipe noses, distribute hugs, encouragement and punishments, stir things up and put matters to rights, absolutely delight me. I've always thought that patriarchs have a little extra something, and that's generosity. It's something a lot of men lack, and I prefer big, warm hearts to great, cold minds.

Mini-poll of men

Paternal vocations, however, are not often to be found. It seems that men like children, and quite like playing daddy, although they don't really know why they should have them or how they ought to bring them up. These uncertainties encourage them to play a waiting game. Unlike the women who, as we've already noted, mostly regret not having had all the children they would have liked, fathers on the whole declare themselves satisfied with the size of their families.

During the course of a mini-poll organized in June 1986 amongst a group of married men running financial committees in the Paris district, we used the same questionnaire as the one in the preceding chapter[1]. The idea was to find out whether men shared the opinions of their wives about how many children they had – it made no difference whether the wives went out to work or stayed at home.

The men's reactions were totally different: *three-quarters of the men questioned considered they had enough children*.

Even men with no children were satisfied with their situation. While nearly all the non-mothers we had come across during our mini-polls had expressed regret, three out of four non-fathers made no complaints about their 'loneliness', even if they were married. Having discussed the matter at a bit more length with our interviewees, all we got was the same reaction: 'One child, that's fine . . . two children, that's fine . . . three children, that's fine . . . WE'RE QUITE CONTENT. There's no doubt, the vast majority of men don't feel their paternal egos are being frustrated!

1. See the comparative questionnaire on page xx. We did our research in the Salon Ecoprise at the Palais des Congrès, Paris. The sample, consisting of about 50 men, had an average age of 41. 85% were married, 84% being fathers. 26% had one child, 38% two children, 20% three or more. These proportions, although not obtained scientifically, are more or less near enough to the usual averages for the answers to be considered as providing a good indication of people's attitudes in 1986.

Well, there it is . . . their cup is three-quarters full of kids who leave no room for male thirst for parenthood! Even so, I've always been taught that you should consider the top and the bottom of a cup to get a complete picture of the situation: that leaves a rather empty quarter. . . . If one man out of four would agree to re-register his surname with the Registry of Births, that would be something. If he then had a second child to keep his only child company, or a third to please his wife who wants it in spite of being worried that it might prove too heavy a burden, there's no doubt that the birthrates of Western nations would be put on their feet again to a man!

We won't discuss it any further, but if I were prime minister, I would entirely change the thrust of this long drawn-out debate on the birthrate. Rather than harping on at women – and only at them – with the same hackneyed expressions about women staying at home with their families, I would direct my remarks slightly more at their husbands and live-in boyfriends in the hope of stimulating their paternal streaks.

Today's young men who feel they've been rather duped by frenzied individualism and the vital importance attached to being successful, might well be open to persuasion. They have the feeling that something is on the move between men and women, and it could end up producing children.

VII

Early Signs Of A Change Of Heart

Christine Ockrent, the star of French television journalism is interviewing Jacques Chirac, leader of the opposition. It's 25 February 1986, three weeks before the elections, important elections which could overturn the majority. Millions of viewers are watching the broadcast at peak viewing time.

Christine Ockrent, who is a real pro, is asking precise questions with her usual beautiful, somewhat predatory smile. She has taken particular care with her appearance – her makeup is perfect, her hairstyle impeccable and she's wearing a roomy, light-coloured sweater which goes perfectly with her eyes. The fact that she's so conscious of her appearance is understandable: it can't be all that easy appearing in front of the cameras when you're more than eight months pregnant. (Her son, Alexander, will be born on 11 March.)

With this book already in mind, I found this journalist's performance altogether courageous and symbolic. Courageous because you need a hell of a lot of determination to worry about your appearance a few weeks before having a baby. It's generally a time when you feel unattractive, with a shapeless figure and blurred features. It's bad enough facing your nearest and dearest when hardly at your best, but to face millions of obviously critical viewers amounts to nothing less than a miraculous performance. (*All* televiewers, especially women, are waiting ready to pounce on the slightest change in appearance when television personalities appear on the small screen. 'Did you notice her new hairstyle?' 'She was better with her hair a bit shorter/ longer.' 'Fancy wearing a striped tie with a check jacket!') When I hear these sort of things it always makes me very sceptical about the impact made by items announced at the beginning of the news, or by the first sentences of televised speeches. Apart from a few people who have no-one to make comments to, I think that practically everyone glued to the television is much busier making remarks about what they're seeing than listening to what they're being told!

Christine didn't have to appear in public a few days before her baby was born. On the contrary, she was officially on maternity leave. Therefore she had quite deliberately decided to show herself in the full bloom of pregnancy. Her appearance was her way of announcing to the world that she was about to be a mother. Millions of girls and young wives must have seen her as a symbol of a particular kind of woman who is adding a new context to motherhood. Politics and pregnancy sounds an unlikely mixture doesn't it?

In fact, for millions of young women, Christine Ockrent is the archetype of a successful career woman in what is traditionally a 'man's world' – the communications sector, which is both prestigious and demanding. She has got to the top of her profession as a journalist without ever letting her private life get in the way. At thirty-five she was still single and childless, like a lot of modern young women who have neither the time nor the inclination to get married and have a family, thereby adding family responsibilities to professional ones.

Ockrent, heavy with child, in full view on the television. Ockrent, showing off her baby to the editor of one of the leading popular magazines – not married to the baby's father, she is proud of the couple formed by herself and her baby. These are classic pictures, mother smiling at the camera, baby wrapped up in shawls with a crumpled little face – but it's not the way that most newscasters tell the world about their babies.

It's absolutely normal for princesses in Britain or Monaco to produce heirs: that's what they're there for. When they're between twenty-five and thirty-five, apart from a few charity galas and official visits, they haven't really got anything else to do except produce two or three princes or princesses to ensure the succession. It's also normal for women married to celebrities, like Mrs McEnroe to want to show off the fruit of their (usually) legal union with the child's famous father – that's also a traditional gesture. On the other hand when women who are leading personalities decide to let their figures go, that's something quite different.

Quite a new angle.

Approaching forty

A whole generation of women between thirty and forty is currently experiencing the desire for a child which they had suppressed, but which is reasserting itself in a most pressing way as they approach their forties. They were twenty years old in the seventies, a period of great protest against the fact that one of the conditions of motherhood was that you had to make sacrifices – you had to give up the idea of a successful career as soon as you 'chose' to have a family. At that time, an investigation of American women students revealed that 6% of young, unmarried women – more amongst those taking higher degrees – declared that they didn't want to have children even if they got married. They felt that their desire for a successful career was incompatible with domestic responsibilities. These dedicated 'career first' women were more common in the United States than in Europe, but these days they are to be found in all the professions and service industries: they're intelligent and attractive, dressed in neat black suits, with their hair cut short and their sights fixed high. They're efficient . . . and a little bit wistful.

In her book about the difficulties of being a mother in modern American society, Sylvia Ann Hewlett, describing a meeting of young women executives, all with Harvard degrees and more than half of whom were still childless at the age of thirty, said:

> 'The tension emanating from these young women really makes an impression on you. They feel they have so little time left to do everything they want to do in life. In spite of their youth, they seem to regard themselves as failures. They feel they're under psychological pressure from all sides, having so much still to do, and so little time to do it in: everything needs to be done *now*. They're worried about whether they'll be able to stay ahead in their careers, but they're equally worried about their 'biological clocks' and whether they will be able to have children before they reach their child-bearing limits. Finally, they're worried about whether they will find a husband, as they see the choice of available men getting narrower every year. They are right to be worried because there is no real place yet in American society for women who have both a family and a career.'

Those responsible for the 'baby flop'

In films and television serials they're always showing women executives in advertising agencies or New York banks; in fact, you find them in most business centres. They're aged between thirty and thirty-five, and for some time now they've been anxiously deliberating on all these problems of career/motherhood, and they tackle these existential matters in a very different way to women of the preceding generation.

My social group, consisting of women born between 1930 and 1940, considered having children to be of the utmost importance. Wanting to be a mother went without saying. From then on, life got more and more complicated for those who wanted to continue their careers. It involved trying to think of new ways of organizing your life and your marriage and of struggling to change business attitudes, to improve women's salaries and to make changes in the law. That generation fought for a lot and did quite well. Nevertheless, to succeed in bringing up a family as well as having a career often proved so exhausting that a lot of the daughters of these hectically busy mothers had no wish to follow their example.

The following social group, those born in the fifties, consciously or subconsciously decided to pursue their studies and consolidate their careers before having any children. As their studies were often long, and establishing a business career is even more of a struggle for girls than it is for boys, they put off their maternal careers till later. It's the daughters of the 'baby boom' who are mainly responsible for the 'baby flop'.

Ten years ago, when I was working in radio, I happened to have two young women colleagues who fitted exactly into this generation of determined non-mothers. They both had mothers who had never worked, and they were both excellently qualified, pretty, ambitious, intelligent and determined girls who, when they were twenty-five years old asserted:

'I'll never have any children. I've no wish to whatsoever. I feel quite feminine enough without needing to be a mother.'

I liked them very much, and their decision not to have children depressed me. I felt just as I would if I met someone who had taken a vow of chastity – sad to know that they would never experience one of the greatest, most important and quite irreplaceable moments that exist in a lifetime. Personally, I would rather die knowing I hadn't missed anything!

The discussions we had on the subject and my defence of motherhood were to no avail – both of them were convinced that they weren't made like me. In their opinion I still belonged to a generation of women who had been brainwashed since childhood to play at dolls' tea parties or being nurses. They maintained they didn't need to play mummies and daddies to achieve complete womanhood.

One of them, Catherine, married a young man who was an individualist like her, and was horrified at the thought of having anything to do with potties, bottles or nappies. The other one, Christiane who, according to her, was even luckier, thoroughly enjoyed her freedom as a woman executive until she fell madly in love with a divorced man with three children.

> 'It's absolutely perfect! I won't need to marry him and give him children. He's got plenty of kids by his first marriage, otherwise we'd have had some serious disagreements as his paternal streak is as hyperactive as my maternal streak is dormant!'

For ten years they both kept their figures and maintained their careers more or less successfully. They had their ups and downs like most people working today. Not having children isn't enough to make a woman earn a fortune or get right to the top!

Anyway, when they were both thirty-five I received two telephone calls, the first one announcing that the wife was pregnant, and the second one announcing that the mistress was going to marry her 'family man' because she wanted to add a half-brother or sister to his brood.

I couldn't resist commenting on their decisions, which had been quite out of the question ten years earlier. They both admitted that the forty-year-old deadline, which was looming on the horizon with its threat that their reproductive system might no longer be functioning well enough to produce a baby, had really been worrying them. Their urge to have a baby had become pressing. I did have one question: would they ever have the time, the courage or the energy to have a second? Both thought not, without being too definite in their estimates. No-one could have convinced them ten years ago that they would one day find themselves with a baby in their arms!

Catherine's baby and Christiane's marriage underlined my conviction that something is going on in the hearts and minds of adults concerning children in general, and the ones that they themselves might have in particular.

A surge of fashion for parenthood

'When my wife is pregnant, I see pregnant women everywhere. I get the impression that amongst my friends and acquaintances more people are getting married and having children. It probably doesn't show up yet in statistics because it's completely the opposite to what you read in the papers. I have a feeling that it's to do with a change of fashion that started off the idea of not marrying or having children fifteen years or so ago!'

This opinion of a father aged thirty-four who was trying to clarify his feeling that a profound change was taking place in the general attitude to the birthrate, was well founded. A sort of surge of fashion for parenthood is just becoming apparent after a fifteen-year period of Malthusianism.

Everywhere I've been, I myself have also picked up early signs of a change of heart, of new developments, a change in values and the search for a different balance.

It's not a question of propaganda or an organized press campaign – rather the reverse. There's a vague atmosphere, little signs which are on the increase, pointing to the fact that people are looking for new ways of being parents. It's as though the arrival of a baby into the world is no longer restricted to the traditional picture we had in our childhood fairy tales: 'They got married and had lots of children.'

Today's young adults seem to have absorbed the crisis in marriage and the traditional family, and are beginning to think of new kinds of behaviour and different motives for having children. In the beginning, faced with marriage break-ups, increases in divorce rates, and the development of common law marriage, they reacted with disillusion and suspicion, casting to the winds traditional morals, white weddings, pink and blue babies and their own red eyes when young couples and their families tore one another to pieces.

Even so, the urge to live as a couple and build a family has gradually recaptured its value. Staying single is a possible solution – and single people are on the increase, but often it's only a stop-gap – it's certainly better to live alone than to be unhappy, but how many people living in peaceful solitude wouldn't swap their tranquillity on the spot for married bliss? Are the millions of men and women who sleep in single beds and dine alone at night with only the television for company happy with their lot? Are they in no hurry because no-one's waiting for them? Then why do 'lonely hearts' columns have the highest readership of the whole press? Why are 'singles clubs' spreading even in quite small towns? You certainly wouldn't want to live with just any old partner, but nevertheless there's a lot to be said for living with someone. Nowadays people's expectations are much more personal, and they're no longer prepared to slide quietly into the groove prepared for them by society's conventions. Everyone has to have his own individual reason for giving in to an instinct which is as old as the hills –to live with someone, have children and organize a family unit which will ensure the survival of all its members.

A return to wedding rings

All options are open, even the most traditional ones. We mustn't forget that, although more people are living together without getting married in countries like Sweden and Denmark, which have always been considered anti-marriage both in their morals and their laws, half of the men and women do still get married.

Incidentally, the number of marriages in Denmark increased in 1984. A report on the subject stated: 'More and more Danes are getting married – marriage is making a come-back. 28624 couples got married in 1984, which is an increase of 1582 over the previous year.'

I made a quick calculation: this figure represents a 6% increase in marriages. Surely that must be a 'sign'? A sign from the north where they carry on in a very avant-garde way with regard to moral standards.

In Europe, changes in lifestyle swing up and down like a pendulum. The Nordic countries were the instigators of the new way of living, and the Central European countries, Holland, England, France, Belgium and Switzerland, followed suit. It took five or ten years more for the Mediterranean countries, Italy, then Spain and Portugal, to join in the dance in their turn. That's what happened with contraception, the decrease in fertility, marriage, divorce, young people living together, etc. If the Danes are putting rings on fingers again, we too shall soon be rediscovering the joys of the wedding feast!

As I would always much prefer to describe my cup as half full rather than half empty, I find the number of young people still getting married in other European countries remarkably high – provided, of course, no comparison is made with statistics for other times and other moral standards! In France and Italy, for instance, which are on their way to becoming the least 'marrying' countries in Western Europe, two-thirds of boys and girls still get married – and two marriages out of three take place in church!

Of those who get married in the eighties, it's estimated that one marriage in two will end in divorce. What amazes me is not that one-third of these couples will separate, but that the other two-thirds hope to stay married for life.[1] Let's hope that the couples remain sufficiently strong and active for such a large proportion of them to withstand the test of time!

All the prevailing circumstances which forced people to live together even when they didn't want to do so – religious laws as well as civil laws, financial constraints as

---

1. A marriage which, because expectation of life gets longer all the time, is increasingly likely to last 40 or 50 years, whereas in the 18th century, the average was 15-20 years.

well as social customs, have slowly disintegrated yet, in spite of that, marriage is still holding its own. It unites men and women and is the most important basis for everyday life. Here is another sign that is worth pointing out.

Eight unusual ways of becoming parents

Apart from the traditional framework of 'legitimate couple/legitimate children' which exists for men and women between twenty-five and thirty and which incidentally results in the classic nuclear family (Daddy + Mummy + two children), we're beginning to see the emergence of more unusual ways of becoming parents – families out of the norm, unforeseen events and family ties which are natural or emotional rather than legitimate. One should note the following, which, though recent, are significant:

1. Acknowledgment of natural children

In the Nordic countries, four babies out of ten are born out of wedlock; in France it was 17.8% in 1985, and in Great Britain, Italy and Spain, babies previously 'illegitimate' and now 'natural' increase in number all the time. The parents don't bother to go to the Registry Office to get married before the baby is born, but very sensibly ensure they carry out all the government formalities when they acknowledge them officially. Eight out of ten natural children born in 1985 were acknowledged by their mothers . . . and their fathers. Incidentally, Mummy, Daddy and the baby all live together. They may sometimes even get married later on, except when Mummy is working and refuses categorically to make a joint tax declaration with Daddy.

2. The about-turn by childless women approaching forty

We've already discussed them at length, but there is one additional point: these childless women in their thirties who have nearly left things too late, often have difficulty finding a would-be father. Most of them are tied up, and those that are divorced aren't in a hurry to get hooked again!

I put this question to Susan who was expecting her first baby at thirty-seven, expressing surprise that she was so late getting down to it:

> 'I've been longing for a child for at least ten years, but I hadn't been able to find a kind, affectionate and available man to share my life and my plans for a family. I've been living for three years with the father of my future baby. He's divorced and already has two children by his first wife. It's taken me all this time to get his consent – I didn't want to spring a baby on him. That's why I'm a rather old mother.'

3. 'Afterthoughts' stage a come-back

Some women, who had their first children very young, give themselves the luxury of an 'afterthought' once they are settled both from a career and a financial point of view. This, if they want to do so, gives them the chance to lie permanently about their age because these days they can have children at an age when their own mothers could only hope to have grandchildren.

This phenomenon is due both to progress in pre-natal medicine and a change in women's attitudes to age. As amniocentesis and termination have almost totally eliminated the risk of abnormal children in late pregnancies, why not, when you get to forty and are firmly established, treat yourself to the third child which you didn't have when you were under thirty and struggling to make your way in life. Being ten years younger both in appearance and zest for life, today's forty-year-old adults take on challenges that their own parents only dared face at thirty. A child late in life is one of these challenges.

Three of my close friends have chosen to do this. They're wild with enthusiasm, and at kindergarten parents' meetings they find themselves rubbing shoulders with young parents who seem to them like their older children. There's only one drawback to which all older mothers admit:

'Our youngest is incredibly badly brought up – or should I say dragged up. His father and I no longer feel as energetic as we did when bringing up the older children. Above all, we've become immensely sceptical about the value of upbringing in general, and our own principals in particular,'[2]

4. Children of second marriages are on the increase

Contrary to popular opinion, divorce is more a creator of children than anything else. New couples want to start new families. We all know of men and women who would never have exceeded the crucial one or two children if they had stayed married to the mother or father of their first-born. In the case of remarriage, or simply of joining up with a new partner – divorced people are even less keen than those who've never been married on legalizing successive love affairs, except in America where they don't mind how many times they cut the wedding cake – the couple often find they want a baby all to themselves as a fulfilment of their new love, never mind how many half-brothers or sisters will be there to greet his arrival.

Children of second marriages who previously were born to young women with middle-aged husbands, are nowadays conceived irrespective of the age difference. Women over thirty-five refuse to allow young women to be the only ones to resort to this old wives' recipe for hanging on to their husbands, especially when the age difference favours the father!

5. Triumphant polygamists

A married man with a family has a child by his mistress. He doesn't want to leave his wife and children, but at the same time he wants to do the right thing by his girlfriend. Whereas before this was an impossible situation, and a

2. It's become quite usual to say that a thirty-year-old woman of Jane Austen's day would correspond with a forty-year-old today. Personally, I wonder when looking at Joan Collins, Elizabeth Taylor, Jane Fonda or Claudia Cardinale whether a fifty-year old isn't the equivalent in mind and spirit of the thirty-year-old of 150 years ago!

source of rows and drama, these alternative forms of paternity have now been legalized in France. A law has recently been passed authorizing fathers to acknowledge their 'bastards'. This liberalism has deeply shocked conservative moralists, but it does, however, have some advantages for the birthrate! Single mothers are more likely not to get rid of a baby that has been acknowledged by the father – they hope, sometimes in vain, that it will help to swing the bigamy balance in their favour.

6. Deliberate single parents

In the old days, society was organized in such a way that single parenthood was shunned. Since then, 'unmarried mothers' have been replaced by 'one parent mothers' – some single women want to have a child even though they're not living with a man. Some women refuse to subject their desire for a child to a man's authority because of rampant militancy. There are fewer and fewer of these women amongst the new generations, who have no need whatsoever to indulge in the sex war to prove their existence. Others quite simply haven't been able to find a partner in the long run, and choose to have a fatherless baby rather than get old all alone.

There's another source of single parenthood: homosexuality. In the States you hear of couples consisting of two mothers or two fathers who long to bring up children together. It's relatively simple for women: one of them can get artificially . . . or naturally inseminated. For men it's much more tricky: they have to resort to adoption, which isn't all that easy because adoption agencies are hardly likely to give priority to homosexuals when deciding who to hand their babies over to. We'd better not rely too much on homosexuals to increase the birthrate!

7. Sterility's multiple pregnancies

Fertility may be on the decline, but sterility is being treated more and more vigorously. The medical methods available to help couples have children are improving all the time. Some results even surpass all patients' expectations, enabling them to produce not one, but often two, some-times three and even occasionally more children. In addition, sterile women who've been cured, are hardly ever content with one child. Amazed at themselves for having been able to get things under way, they're more tempted than others to renew the experience. It's like the story I was told about a young woman's venture into motherhood. She was sterile at thirty and a mother of four at thirty-three: her son was presented with three little sisters on the same day!

8. Adoptions by couples who want a child to love

When you can't have the child you long for, you try to find ways of pouring out your love on to one that has already been born. Sadly, there aren't enough unwanted babies on our side of the world to satisfy demand, so you have to go an increasingly long way to find them. There's no problem in assimilation for these mini-immigrants – they immediately become part and parcel of the population and of the statistics for children per couple.

Bifurcation: birthrate/depopulation

Even if you add up all those children outside the traditional framework of the nuclear family, they won't make up for the deficit in the birthrate, but a diversity of motives and circumstances creates a new sphere of influence which will have the effect of reintegrating children into people's plans for the future, and this could well mark the end of the great drop in the birthrate.

Organizations that sound out European public opinion on socio-cultural matters have noticed it.[3] Observers in seventeen Western countries have made a study of the various possible 'bifurcations' in areas where big changes may occur in the fairly near future in all Western nations.

1. Depopulation or rise in the birthrate.
2. Weakening or strengthening of the economy.

3. Courcheval seminary (13–19 April 1985) of all the members of the R.I.S.C. (Research Institute on Social Change).

3. A new paradigm inspired by current scientific thinking or, conversely, determined by future discoveries in neuro-science and some radically new sides to reality.

Sociologists differ in their judgement on the first point, which we're dealing with here, from the usual lamentations. Although they acknowledge that the most up-to-date prognoses are generally extremely pessimistic, they don't consider that the slide towards depopulation is fatal. They account for their relative optimism in the following way:

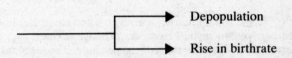

Depopulation

Rise in birthrate

'The possibility of favourable development in European demography rests on the two following observations:-
– Women who are in tune with social and cultural changes are no longer concentrating on fighting against men for supremacy, but rather on ways and means of widening their scope and being creative in doing things their own way.
– At the same time there is less tendency for women to look on themselves and their lives as one indivisible unit. You can be "yourself" in successive and different ways, by having several careers, etc . . . You don't need to choose between being either a mother or a career woman. It's possible that women's lives will develop in such a way that they will have phases of motherhood and phases of professional, intellectual or artistic fulfilment. It could become accepted practice to arrange your life so that you bring up three children successfully and at the same time have a career which is organized in such a way that these two ambitions do not get in each other's way.

Seen like this, any initiative which would allow flexibility in work could turn out to be essential, and could reveal latent ambitions. We must not forget that socio-cultural development can never be straightforward. Cofremca[4] and R.I.S.C. have, in the last ten years, often had the opportunity of bringing to light a system in which there are three successive phases, in a particular order: you follow the norm; then you rebel; finally, you release creative expression. In the particular case of the birthrate, creative expression is synonymous with reconciling work and motherhood.'

Work and motherhood aren't easy to reconcile, I hear career women saying! Even so, a change of heart isn't the exclusive property of the rising generation. Those belonging to it weren't born under the old regime and don't need to question the established order because they themselves have been brought up in an atmosphere of fairly chaotic change, and they will probably feel the need to strengthen the emotional ties which hold people together because they feel perfectly free. Too free perhaps, a bit fed up with all this permissiveness and cult of the individual which they've had enough of.

The generation of caring women

After the generation of dutiful women, followed by the generation of liberated women, caring women can just be seen peeping over the horizon of the year 2000. It goes without saying that loving spells child, or even children. Whether you like to admit it or not, these little things are the most amazing (practically automatic) dispensers of love there have ever been – don't you agree?

When I started writing this book, I really was afraid that I was swimming against the tide with my ideas on children. As my investigations have gone on, I have begun

4. French correspondent of R.I.S.C.

to regain hope. No, I'm not completely out of date when I dream of little eager faces and tables crowded with children. Perhaps I'm even ahead of my time. There are others beside myself who are beginning to understand why child*ren* looks better than child when it's written in the Golden Book.

VIII

Never Have One Without A Second

'There is a well known formula for paediatrics which goes: "A mother's heart grows bigger according to the number of children she has". It's good and very apt. The more children you have, the more love you have to give. These days, most households can afford to have three children. They may not be over-indulged, but is that such a bad thing? The parents' job is to love their children and to provide them with everything they need. But everything they need doesn't mean everything they want . . .'

'An only child's parents have more time to themselves, and therefore they find it easier to follow their cultural pursuits . . . It's the process of continually having to care for young children who are born one after the other that makes a mother get used to a limited and non-intellectual world . . .'

The first quotation is from Edwige Antier, a French paediatrician who proclaims the advantages of families which aren't necessarily large, but do at least have more than one child. The second is from Ellen Peck, an American psychologist whose book, as its title suggests – *The Only Child – Well Balanced Child, Happy Parents* – is a sincere plea to restrict your family to one child.

It would be easy to go on for ever quoting opinions and

recommendations by child specialists in this debate on the advantages or otherwise of only children. In articles and manuals on child psychology you find completely contradictory opinions. Some child psychologists, like Professor Robert Debré (one of the founders of modern paediatrics) have always maintained that the only child was a 'being apart', constantly overwhelmed by the whole array of gestures, attentions, anxieties and care lavished on him as a result of his parents' joint protective instincts. Others, such as Jean-Pierre Almodovar maintain the reverse, that an only child behaves in exactly the same way in school and at home as his friends who have brothers and sisters.

Sole depository for all their ambitions

Careful observation of only children, carried out mainly by American researchers, has revealed that the scholastic and university results achieved by those high flyers who always come top of their year are often due to the fact that they, as only children, are the sole depository for all their parents' ambitions. Also, as they are the only ones to benefit from the large sums of money put aside to pay for their studies and subsidize their student expenses, they can swot for their exams without having to worry about money, which is not the case for students who come from large families.

The woman with the highest IQ in the world, an American called Marilyn Mach vos Savant, on the other hand attributes her IQ of 230 to the fact that she was brought up in a family of three.

> 'I've always been eager to learn. When I was a child I was desperately keen to understand everything . . . My parents both worked, so I pestered my brothers continually. When I was five I thought just like them although they were twelve and thirteen.'

An exception to the rule which says that little geniuses stay quietly in their single rooms with their desks all to themselves, and where no-one touches their things and there are no brothers or sisters to pinch their rubbers or crayons!

In fact, an endless argument has been going on between psychologists and demographers for more than a century, with everyone reaching his own conclusions based on personal experience and professional observations. However, a tendency towards moderation seems to have been emerging from recent studies. The only child is no longer to be considered inevitably 'handicapped' as had been proclaimed before (incidentally, more for moral reasons inspired by the well known phrase 'go forth and multiply' than for scientific ones). He's certainly not considered 'bad' any more, but different nevertheless. Jacqueline Dana described him very well:

> 'What is an only child? Simply a child without any brothers or sisters. That doesn't mean that he's going to develop any special characteristics associated with being an only child – each one has his own family history, heredity, qualities and defects. Each one is different, and it would be inept and unfair to try and give them a narrow definition which doesn't correspond with reality . . . quite simply, the only child's family circumstances are different to those of other children. What matters most is why he is an only child. It is fundamentally important to make a distinction between those who are only children as a result of a deliberate decision, and those whose uniqueness was beyond the parents' control . . .'

Only child or first child with no successor

To sum up once more, it's not so much a question of the children being a bit more like this, or a bit less like that, but rather their parents' attitude. Obviously, a couple who deliberately restrict their family to one child aren't behaving in the same way as a couple who want lots of children but are unable to have more than one. Certainly, the latter are much more parents in spirit than the former, and the child probably finds them easier to get on with because he therefore isn't an 'only' child but a 'first child with no successor'.

A paediatrician once said to me:

'We always have the feeling that of all our patients it's the only children who come to us most often for consultations. In my opinion, this doesn't necessarily point to a greater degree of physical or psychological weakness on the part of the child himself, but rather to greater anxiety on the part of the parents, particularly the mother. Incidentally, I can almost guess my small patients' place in the family from the number of times they come to see me each year. The more children there are in a family, the less visits they make to the doctor. Mainly because the parents have acquired the experience to enable them to cope more easily with little routine illnesses, but also because their anxiety is divided between several children.'

We really should talk about death

When discussing anxiety and the only child we must face up to death. When we discuss children, we no longer even consider their death because we're lucky enough to be able to have a fantastic number of children who are sure to survive us. This is a very recent phenomenon which has been in existence for barely a century. We never normally discuss the possibility of a child dying, even amongst husbands and wives or very close family. This is because we live in a society which tries to banish death by every possible means, as though blotting it out of our minds will prevent it happening. Even so, which of us parents can say we don't often think about it in relation to our children, whatever age they may be. Elderly parents don't lose this anxiety – on the contrary, if anything they have more time to spare on turning their hair white!

We really have no immediate reason to dread our children's death more than our own – if anything, we should dread it less: statistically, children run much less risk of dying than adults, but that doesn't stop us suffering a thousand agonies every day. Our anxiety knows no bounds as soon as a child:

- pushes a thermometer above 40° or 104°, as the Anglo-Saxons used to say. Antibiotics or not, we're haunted by memories of our own childhood when our temperatures reached this degree which, however, is no longer considered a serious symptom;
- hides for longer than five minutes in a cupboard or at the end of the garden – we immediately imagine him run over, drowned or abducted by a sex maniac;
- doesn't get home in time for his favourite television serial – we immediately imagine him . . . (see above);
- rings us at the office at lesson-time;
- eats 'nothing' for two days. Or, to be more accurate, eats what we consider to be 'nothing', but which generally is quite enough to keep him from starvation, even if it isn't enough to ensure proper growth;
- doesn't let us know how he is when on holiday even though he's with a well supervised group, but is just as impossible to get hold of on the telephone as we are ourselves;
- sets off on a journey no matter what time, season, distance or method of transport. This source of worry is inexhaustible and justified. Even when you're thirty or forty you should *never* tell your parents the exact time you plan to leave point A, otherwise they will get themselves into a state three minutes after the time you're due at point B.

This anxiety, caused by the fear of death, doesn't annoy anyone when you are discreet about it, but it poisons children's lives when parents allow it to get the better of them and it infuriates children who feel literally persecuted by it. One of my grandmothers beat all the records for worrying. Every time her daughters or her grandchildren left the house she would warn them 'Take care of yourselves!' All her life we implored her to get rid of this obsession, but she never managed to.

Having had to put up with this harassment myself, I swore that I wouldn't be over-protective in this way towards my own children, by giving in to my morbid maternal fears. To be quite honest, my attitude leaves a lot to be desired. I'm almost as scared, but I don't let anyone know about it so often. All the same, I often hear myself saying to the children as they're getting into the car: '*Do* be careful not to drive too fast, and phone me as soon as you get there!' They smile, trying not to look too irritated and mutter 'OK, I'm listening!' Just let them wait a few years till their own children have passed their driving tests – then we'll see whether they sleep soundly while their children are on the road!

Obviously, an only child who has to put up with all his parents' morbid fears is much more conscious than other children of the heavy burden his irreplaceable value places on him. I recently met a mother whose only son of eighteen had just been killed in a motorcycle accident. I have never seen anyone so near to total despair. I got the impression that she needed to talk about her distress even to someone she didn't know, like myself, just to stop herself going mad. She repeated several times:

> 'To think that my husband and I only wanted one child so that we'd be able to give him everything – including a motorbike. I've kept on asking myself since he left us (she never used the word "died"): if only we'd had several children we couldn't have afforded to buy it for him. Perhaps he'd still be here. In any case, we wouldn't have been left all alone, with no-one to give anything to . . .'

The Catherine generation

In the only children v. several children debate, parents' convictions turn out to be just as strong as those of the sociologists and psychiatrists. All the parents I questioned defended their decisions fiercely to try and justify logically what everyone knows quite well are purely personal, emotional reactions produced by their subconscious, family histories and plans for the future.

'In our family, a second child would have made things very complicated – life would have become a balancing act! A child takes up a lot of his parents' time so, bearing in mind our two careers, we decided to give up any idea of a second child, telling each other that it just wasn't sensible. You can't have children if you don't have the time for them! Parents can give an only child a much larger share of everything.' (Catherine, thirty-three years old, shopkeeper, mother of one daughter aged eleven.)

'A second child has always seemed essential to me, even though I'm a mother on her own. An only child and a mother on her own – particularly a boy and his mother, as in my case, are almost bound to have a hothouse relationship with the result that they get on each other's nerves, whereas a mother plus two children, even if she is single, adds up to a family. You shouldn't have a child unless you are prepared to have a proper family and give him a brother or sister.' (Catherine, forty years old, a PE teacher and mother of three. Having got married after her two sons were born, she was no longer single when her third child arrived.)

It's quite by coincidence that the two mothers I came across during my research and have quoted from here both happen to be called Catherine. I've deliberately kept to this name because it's very popular among the present generation of French child-bearing women. Catherines don't just rush blindly into having children, they always find good arguments to justify their decisions to have a family. They go into the pros and cons of each one, backing them up with facts. They display remarkable subjectivity when trying to convince you that *objectively*-speaking their conclusion was the only viable one in the circumstances.

It's impossible not to give the example of two families whose annual incomes with two salaries coming in, were exactly the same: £15,000, give or take a few pounds. The first couple justified their decision to have only one child by giving their joint income as the reason: they maintained it wasn't large enough to ensure a reasonable living standard for a family of four. The second couple was equally convinced that their joint income was enough to cover the expenses of their two children, although they felt that having a third would definitely have upset their budget. Everything is relative! – especially when you tackle the two most widely discussed and least universally shared subjects: money and children.

The Collange conviction

Why should I seem to be more objective than others in this debate? I don't pretend to be the least bit impartial. I do have an opinion – more than that even – a conviction, which I shall do my best to share with all the Catherines who read this book and their companions, official and unofficial.

THE COLLANGE CONVICTION: **Never have one without a second. No-one in the world can force someone else to have children. The right not to be a parent is one of an individual's fundamental freedoms. Having said that, you shouldn't have a child unless you have made a definite decision to have at least two. An only child is a selfish present that parents give themselves for all sorts of egocentric and complicated reasons. Two children represent a family that you give to each of them . . . and to yourselves as parents at the same time.**

Yes, I know the saying 'a bird in the hand is worth two in the bush'. It's very apt for sweets, flats, salaries, jobs and even long-lasting love affairs, but it won't do for children.

I'm quite convinced that for *all* children it's far more

instructive, entertaining, pleasant and important not to be the only one. In spite òf scraps, jealousies, unfairness, lies, tale-telling, complexes, frustrations, mutual incompatibilities, parental preferences[1] (and those of brothers and sisters), the arrival of a second or third child and so on, is of the greatest possible value to the first.

In spite of everything that makes him cry into his pillow at night – although life is bound to be 'unfair' more often than it should, and the innocent inevitably land up being punished – although your share of the cake is obviously smaller when it's cut into six instead of four, and the older children always get the new clothes, and although shared rooms destroy privacy, I have never met anyone who regretted his childhood with brothers and/or sisters, whereas the opposite opinion is frequently expressed.

Injustice, spitefulness, confrontations that arise from living in a group and unfair shares are all a part of growing up. Later on, in your career, your social life and emotional relationships you will have to face up to inequalities and harassments which are inherent in all human society. It's by having brothers and sisters, not only parents, that you learn to stick together and stand up to these sorts of things.

Have a good look round you – you will hardly ever find only children who are themselves the parents of only children. Sometimes they don't have any children at all, but much more often they do everything they possibly can to prevent anyone else experiencing the loneliness they felt in their childhood.

Divorce isn't so hard on several children

The trio formed by two parents and an only child doesn't make a well balanced family – incidentally, all life's trios

1. Parents who pretend not to have preferences for one or other of their children aren't strictly honest. It's natural to be particularly drawn to one or other of your children, just as you prefer a particular brother, sister or classmate. Preference doesn't entail privilege or exclusiveness.

are equally hellish, whether in work or in love – eternal triangles only work in films! In a trio, it's always a question of three's company, two's none.

As the 'tripod' stands upright, all the parents' marital upsets turn into a nightmare for the only child. It's often said that young people have few children because they are afraid of the insecurity divorce entails. If there is a separation, the only child finds himself bearing the brunt of his parents' dejection, bitterness and heartbreak all on his own. Inevitably egocentric, he had quite naturally considered himself the centre of the couple formed by his parents. Therefore, the slightest disagreement between them makes him feel guilty because he feels it's his fault.

From personal experience, I know that divorce is a thousand times more bearable for two children, who still have interests in common, and can form a group capable of carrying on discussions and preserving some of their own habits quite independently of their parents' broken relationship. An only child can't laugh when he sees his mother crying and his father looking gloomy. Two children can easily forget grown-ups' tears and depressions when they're playing, talking, eating and sleeping together.

Whatever they do, parents are always grown-ups, and they can never entirely share children's games, jokes and way of life however hard they try. Brothers and sisters can, wonderfully well.

The other day I watched a young mother playing Happy Families with her little girl. She was obviously trying hard, but she wasn't really on the same wavelength. In spite of all her kindness, her way of thinking and playing were a grown-up's. She got annoyed when her daughter didn't begin by grabbing everything she had asked for as soon as it was her turn. She all but turned the game into a maths lesson! She was bored and the child wasn't having any fun either.

Children need children. Even their fights can be good for them because they help them to get rid of their aggressiveness.

The 'big jobs' joke

Above all, you need to have several children so they can learn to laugh with each other. Everyone with lots of brothers and sisters will tell you that their childhood memories are interspersed with uncontrollable attacks of the sort of childish giggles that parents can't understand, and don't want to because they find them stupid.

Does BIG JOBS make you laugh? It doesn't me. I'll even admit that hearing those words repeated over and over again by my three grandchildren, shrieking with laughter makes me seriously doubt: 1) their intellectual faculties; 2) their balanced state of mind, which seems distinctly lavatorial to me; 3) the advantage of sending them to school so young, when from the moment they start kindergarten they learn to use the words BIG JOBS as a never-ending source of amusement. However, it seems that 'big jobbery' is indispensable in early childhood with partners of your own generation who appreciate the irresistible wit of these magic utterances!

To that, most parents of only children will reply that brothers or sisters aren't the only possible partners for sharing secrets, discoveries and silly jokes. There are all their little friends, classmates, holiday acquaintances and, most of all, lots of cousins who have all the advantages of brothers and sisters – minus their constant presence. Fantastic – you invite them when your little darling needs amusement, and then you send them back to their parents so that calm is restored to your pocket-sized family.

I wonder if these cousin-borrowers have ever thought that if two only children marry each other there will never be any uncles, aunts and cousins, and no family gatherings or family holidays other than nuclear family ones. If we pursue this argument to its logical conclusion, once we have got rid of large families, perhaps there's a danger, if all the Western nations follow the Germans' example, of finding ourselves in a cousin-free society in the next century. It really won't be much fun to be a child in that brave new world!

Catherine and John: afraid of a second child

In fact, one thing really worries me about the 'Catherine generation': the significant, growing proportion of parents with only children. This doesn't refer to people's intentions, but to the facts. When you question men and women about the size of an ideal family, all the surveys give two or three children as the most popular number. Reality, however, falls well short of people's ideals. In 1983 a poll on the falling birthrate asked two questions which illustrate this contradiction perfectly:

1st question: In your opinion, how many children should there be in an ideal family?
    Ideal number: 2.5.
2nd question: How many children do you have yourself?
    Actual number: 1.7.

All in all, it seems as though the Catherines and their Johns are firm believers in the advantages of bringing up a large family, but don't have the courage of their convictions.

At the present time, the commonest type of family – in West Germany obviously – but equally in France and many other European countries, is the trio of Mummy/Daddy/ only child. The figures for France surprised even me. When repeating over and over again that families should be asked to have a 'third', I stupidly thought that they already had at least two. I was wrong! There are more parents with only children than with two children:

Number of mothers according to the number of children (0 to 24 years) in the family
    1 child .... 3,472,100 mothers
    2 children .... 3,084,100 mothers
    3 children .... 1,312,720 mothers
    4 children .... 421,180 mothers
    5 children or more .... 279,840 mothers

Seven million adults – men and women – preferred not to take the plunge and have a second child because they were afraid of disrupting their lives and of upsetting their budgets which had already been thrown out by the birth of the first child. If only one out of ten of these men and women could have been persuaded to improve their taste for parenthood and risk having another child, the birthrate problem would have been solved for several years!

For the parents' enjoyment as well

Exactly, we can try and explain to them they're wrong. Becoming a parent is complicated, disruptive and difficult. I admit that from that day on one's whole life has to be reorganized in a completely different way. There's no more independence of mind or tranquil selfishness of youth. When you have a child you become a different person.

However, once you have absorbed this initial change, the process from *one* to *two* is much gentler. The children will soon be sharing the same life, the same room, the same back seat in the car and the same craze for the same cartoons provided, of course, that there isn't more than three years between them. . . . Today's young parents tend to have longer gaps between their children. I'm convinced that rather than simplifying their lives by doing this, they make them more complicated.

You can see that I always come back to my conviction: 'Never have one without a second'. Earlier on I meant it as benefiting the children. I'd like to go further and put it to parents that this rule can equally apply to their enjoyment, their happiness, their peace of mind and their freedom. Unlike only children, you never leave several children quite alone when you go out. Whether you go out in the evening for dinner with friends, have a romantic early night, stay in bed late on Sunday morning, practise some kind of sport that's unsuitable for small children or escape for three days to Florence over the May bank holiday, you will have much less of a guilty conscience if you leave behind two or three children.

Mummy or Daddy, or both, can come home from the office later when brothers and sisters keep each other company after school. Even if they squabble, stop each other from doing their homework, complain bitterly the moment their parents get home or create absolute mayhem in the sitting room, you feel much less guilty returning home late to a noisy, cluttered shambles than to a solitary televiewer, his key still on a string round his neck.

Having several children also allows parents to divide up the emotional hazards, disillusionments and sexes, and not demand all the qualities and all the achievements from only one source for every kind of bonus.

Finally, the miracle of a large family! The wide variety in results of the same upbringing on different children who have eaten at the same table each day and listened to their parents voicing the same principles (damn' rubbish, they often think!) eases your conscience, as it demonstrates the uselessness of upbringing in general and your own in particular.

I can just imagine my despair if one of my children had been an only one. Lost in the crowd, his problems with work, society, time-keeping and money have certainly worried me, but they haven't finished me off. With no other reference for my upbringing capabilities, I wouldn't have had either the courage or the wish to write a single line about parent/child relationships.

No, I promise you, you mustn't be content with only one fragile tiny baby whose defencelessness makes you feel so protective, only one six-month-old with his adorable dimples and trusting eyes, only one tottering twelve-month-old trying out his first steps between your loving but not always reliable arms, only one two–four-year-old whose every word is a victory and every look a conquest. I could go on like this until ten or twelve years old, recalling each incredible moment, never quite the same for each child, but never completely different either.

Try it out several times over – be devils!

In spite of all the problems they give you, I'm sure that you will never regret having put body and soul into producing a beautiful collection of individual works of art made entirely of flesh and blood.

And since a spirit of enterprise is once again abroad these days, don't let's forget the attractions of a small family business.

IX

Those Going Into The 'Family Business'

Work and children have lots of things in common:

● When you have too much of either, it's exhausting, and it's wearing on the nerves and the health. When you get to the end of the day, you feel you've just about got the energy to go to bed, only to have to get up again the next morning and face the same old routine and overwork (caused by your job or by the children).

● When there isn't any, you get depressed. You feel empty and useless, with no job to do. Other people round you are busy organizing things and making plans for the future while you yourself have no idea what tomorrow may bring. You'd give anything to have some (work or children).

● When you're lucky enough to find the right balance, it adds a new dimension to your life and makes it exciting, interesting and stimulating. It gives you both personal fulfilment and the opportunity to mix with congenial people in your daily life.

For a very long time, work and children were considered the two worst afflictions a human being could endure. Such prospects as bread earned by the sweat of your brow or the agony of childbirth were hardly cheerful!

Now and again some crank would get pleasure from his work, or a pair of eccentrics would insist that they were happy, relaxed parents, but no-one took them seriously – most people actually distrusted such bad examples, and greatly disapproved of anyone who got pleasure from something that was considered a duty.

You had virtually no choice over your work, and even less over your children. As a rule, the harder your job was, the more children you had. The two afflictions went hand in hand!

Progress swings like a pendulum

In modern times public-spirited, radically-minded people have rebelled against the double 'slavery' of work and children. They have demanded laws to protect workers from unreasonable employers, and parents from the excesses of nature.

They have succeeded in their demands: working hours have been shortened, conditions have been improved, and abortion and contraception have been legalized. Young people have, in the second half of the 20th century, had a reaction against man's exploitation by man, and women's exploitation by children, and have proclaimed the virtues of an individualistic and pleasure-seeking society, with the result that work and children have been completely devalued. The less you work and have children, the more you can get out of life.

However, changing values, mentalities and lifestyles swing back and forth continually like a pendulum. If you want to make people more forward looking, the first thing you do is suggest radically different ideas to them. At the beginning, people are excited by the 'novelty', which they find daring – they plunge in headlong, forgetting everything that went before. Then, when they try to put the new theories into practice, they come up against a blank wall made up of daily habits and realities, and the bright ideas tend to fizzle out. They start questioning everything all over again, making comparisons and being disappointed, and they realize that they needn't have thrown the babies out with the bathwater. The pendulum begins to swing back a bit, but it has gone a long way and doesn't quite get back to its starting point. When change is taken up by the majority, it becomes progress, and it is no longer the sole prerogative of an avant-garde minority.

Over the last twenty years, that's exactly what's happened whenever we have taken part both actively and passively in questioning the established order. Having first of all exploded the theories which almost entirely dominated our lives, we are gradually rediscovering certain unalterable basic essentials: sex, yes, but not without love. Feminism, certainly, but not the sex war. Individualism, all right, but not selfishness, etc.

Everyone wants to take risks

The area in which there has been the most spectacular about-turn in recent years is work, or rather the professions. After the great rush to opt out, when people refused to get involved in the work scene in case it prevented them from devoting their lives to personal fulfilment, the balance has once again tipped in favour of effort, initiative and responsibility at every level. How dated the hippies and flower people of the sixties look when compared with today's high flyers, workers who take over their bankrupt factories and young people who start up in business!

Suddenly, everyone is wanting to exploit his ideas, develop his capabilities, take risks and start up a business even if it means slogging away in a small way to begin with, without the security of belonging to a large organization.

When I think of all that has been said or written in the media about the resurgence of the small businessman, I feel that the merits and qualities of the parent should be the subject of just as much attention. They're exactly the same.

When you have a child, you are truly creating something – you are going into business in the noblest possible way, not for immediate gain, but for the satisfaction of building up something now that will last longer than you will yourself. It's the most selfless investment – very long term, with no guaranteed dividends even though the benefits could be unlimited if all goes well!

If you are a nine-to-five civil servant, someone who takes a back seat in life or finds life too much of a struggle and is apprehensive of the future, stay safely cocooned in the cosy tranquillity of your solitary bachelorhood or your childless marriage. You're not made to be parents.

On the other hand, if you're full of the spirit of enterprise that we keep being told has revived in the last few years – if you'd rather roll up your sleeves than fold your arms and give up, if you think it's more rewarding to invest than to hoard, more satisfying to give than to receive, more exhilarating to take risks than to live safely – you have all the necessary qualities for having children.

Rules for success

For those about to embark on the business of parenthood, here are a few rules to follow to ensure the maximum chance of success. They have nothing to do with advice on the upbringing or development of children – there are hundreds of books on these subjects by psychologists who have much more faith in their principles than I have in mine. They are just a few suggestions to help parents set up in the 'family business' without too much difficulty. Parenthood should become an adventure for everyone now that it is no longer an inevitability.

1. Bear in mind your temperament

Good mothers and fathers have a particular kind of temperament – they are generally much busier than the average person. I've always noticed on my travels, attending conferences, etc, that if you are dealing with charitable organizations or non-profit making associations, the organizers, guides, drivers who fetch you from the station and those in charge of all the arrangements, generally have two or more children. This is particularly noticeable amongst women: the more children they have (planned ones, of course!), the more enthusiastically they throw themselves into professional, social or cultural activities. I know that doesn't in any way correspond with their generally accepted image. But, from having seen it dozens of times, I'm quite convinced that the exceptional energy and vitality displayed by some mothers of large families is part of their innermost nature. Having lots of children is only one way of using it up!

Anne B., a fashion designer with more than twenty shops in various places, and no less than five children, is a typical example of this sort of contemporary woman. She admits to a boundless appetite for the joys of life:

> 'I adore lots of things. I'm very greedy. I'm very attached to the country – I love our house in the Gard. I adore painting – I've done a lot of classical drawing in the art gallery in Versailles. I adore the cinema. I adore New York – each time I go there I come back more in love with it than before. I adore anything that brings happiness. Children . . . happy, carefree moments . . . fulfilment . . .'

What a superb way of declaring your love of life!

In fact, children don't change parents or alter their behaviour; they exhaust the wary, but exhilarate the energetic – if you're a worrier they add to your discomfort, but if you are happy they fill you with joy; they emphasize dissension, but they strengthen bonds.

Therefore, you can't count on children to bring you happiness unless there are other sources of it as well. They won't make you laugh if you don't enjoy life.

On the other hand, those who don't mind not being perfect, who wake up looking forward to the day, who can see beyond the end of their noses and manage to sleep when they're tired should have another child more often.

2. Choose a good business partner

In the old days, men and women got married mainly for
material reasons. The rich tried to find others who were
rich, and the poor looked for a willing pair of hands.
Marriage really was a manufacturing concern. It was more
important for a woman to be a competent housewife than to
have fine personal qualities, and it was more important for
a man to be a tireless worker than to be a good companion.

I've always loved the sort of proposals you get in
Westerns when the cowboy comes back and says, 'For years
I've been looking for someone who can make hot, strong
coffee when I get home. At last I guess I've found you . . .'
and the lady being given this 'compliment' has tears in her
eyes when she realizes that she's finally found a strong
shoulder to lean her delicate head on!

Later on, a man would choose a good-natured, thrifty,
loving and faithful wife, and a woman a strong, hard-
working, courageous and honest husband, thus forming a
couple with all the qualities needed for an unbreakable
union. You had to stay together all your lives – there was no
question of changing your minds if you found out you had
made a mistake.

More recently still, the choice has tended to be for a
sexual partner to share your bed and your physical passion
for as long as possible, who is attractive to look at,
seductive and highly sexed.

The qualities needed to be a good parent are hardly
ever taken into account when it comes to choosing a
partner. Apart from a few famous people who are obsessed
with their succession, either because of their name or their
fortune, the vast majority of today's lovers never even
consider having children when they decide to live together.

It's a pity, because it's more important than ever to
have a child by someone you want to be the mother or
father of your baby and then to share your little boy or girl
and your adolescents, post-adolescents, young adults and
so on for the whole of your life.

Couples are getting more and more vulnerable, and

the chance of growing old together gets increasingly remote,[1] which is why there is more reason than ever to take great care when choosing the man or woman who will be your collaborator in the business of having children. It's vital not to launch into such a venture with just anyone. Even if you change partners at some stage in your life, you must never be ashamed to say to your child, 'When we both decided we wanted to have you, we felt completely bound up in one another and very, very happy. We were in love, and we wanted you to be a bit like both of us.'

Incidentally, just wanting someone to be the mother or father of your child is as good a criterion as any other for choosing a partner. These criteria include reasonable physical qualities (good enough health and appearance to ensure that any resemblance won't be too terrible), satisfactory intellectual faculties (no-one wants a stupid child), and a basic moral sense (although this is the least likely characteristic to be passed on genetically, on the whole one would rather not produce children likely to turn into rats or bitches). Matchmakers weren't so wrong when they used to say that 'good fathers make good husbands'.

3. Don't wait too long

Degree studies and babies don't go well together. While the former are going on, the latter are put to the back of the mind, especially when it's the other's studies we're talking about. Because more and more young women are taking long courses, in future mothers will very probably have their older children when they're between twenty-five and thirty, not between twenty and twenty-five.

In the past, it was considered better to have children when you were young, and had the energy to bring them up well. I think that such theories date from a different age, when conditions of hygiene weakened everyone's health

---

1. Current divorce rates are: one out of three marriages in France, four out of ten in Great Britain and one out of two in the United States and the Scandinavian countries.

from the age of thirty onwards. Couples were encouraged to have children when they were young and healthy and didn't run the risk of dying and leaving orphans at an early age.

Nowadays life is long, and people are as strong and healthy between thirty and forty as they are between twenty and thirty, so why not enjoy your freedom in your twenties before taking on the responsibility of a family? A mother who starts nearer thirty than twenty-five has plenty of time to have two or three children without rushing or getting too tired, and without the slightest risk to her health.

I'm not saying that everyone should go further and follow the example of Marlene Jobert or Ursula Andress.[2] Successful entrepreneurs generally take off at about thirty when they're full of youthful energy and still have plenty of time ahead of them to expand their businesses. It's the same thing for children: a family embarked on too late runs the risk of never reaching its full potential, which brings us back to only children (see the preceding chapter).

Don't start too late, but above all don't wait too long between children: when there's an age difference of less than three years, the advantages are so considerable that they make up for the inconvenience of having a second pregnancy too soon after the first.

I have a very personal observation to make on this question of age. Having had my first child at twenty-one and the second a year later to the day, I cursed for ages at being a mother so young. As a result, I've always advised other young women to enjoy themselves for a few years when they're young before taking on the responsibility of a family. There's a right time for everything, and I can't see any point in playing mummy until you're twenty-five. It wasn't until recently that I've been handed an unexpected bonus – because I was a precocious mother, I find myself a premature grandmother.

2. Marlene Jobert had twin girls (Eva and Joy) at thirty-eight, and Ursula Andress had her first child at forty-two.

Mine hadn't even finished being children before their own joined in the relay race. It's a marvellous way of forgetting your age, because all the generations mingle and are able to enjoy the good things of life together.

Because of contraception and their careers, there's no way that young women of today will be able to enjoy the status of being track-suited grannies. I'm sorry for them because it's enormous fun.

4. Getting off to a difficult start

Getting started in anything, no matter what it is, requires a tremendous effort. This is particularly true of the 'family business'.

I know, tiny babies cry at night and sleep in the day and are merciless towards their parents, who are so drugged with sleep that they don't know which of them is too shattered to ask the other one to get up. But at the worst it only lasts for three or four months.

I know, babies either have toothache or tummyache, or both at once, and they give heartrending cries which upset you and get on your nerves night and day to such an extent that you wonder which of you is too shattered to ask the other to go and quieten the yells. But, at the worst, it only lasts for a year.

I know, when they get to eighteen months, they start being naughty, they touch everything, put everything in their mouths and reach for everything hot, breakable, sharp or dangerous, fall down when they're trying to run and generally drive those responsible for them mad in every possible way. But, at the worst, it only lasts for two years.

After the first twenty-four months, their pattern of life becomes a bit less hectic, and you begin to be able to reason with them. It's important to be honest about all this because it's generally when the first child is at his or her most exhausting that you have to start thinking about having the next one.

I'm always amazed at the way magazines for parents

show practically nothing else but photos of nude babies at their mother's breasts. Frankly, that's a very limited view of parenthood. If the really important moments only occur in early babyhood, I'm not at all sure that it's worth being pregnant for nine months and wracked with insomnia for three more just to sample the delights of tiny babies.

Fortunately, once the tricky period of early upbringing is over, the years of childhood in the real meaning of the word are a source of change, of discovery and of creativeness as rewarding as they are varied – right up till the dreaded arrival of adolescence. I maintain that all those years – plus those you share with your children much later on once they have grown up, are an extremely profitable return on your original investment!

5. Take advantage of modern technology

In matters such as buying new equipment or deciding on new ways of the day-to-day running of the household, techniques develop so rapidly that in order to keep abreast of them, you have to update your skills and be prepared to learn all the time. This is just one more area in which traditional know-how can no longer be handed on. Grannies are quite obsolete if they still believe in:
- hand-knitted matinee jackets;
- bibs which need to be boiled;
- sheets and blankets;
- little girls in pink and little boys in blue;
- vegetables which have to be peeled and passed through a sieve;
- children who have to stay in bed when they have a temperature . . .

I could go on adding to this list indefinitely. Technology has made such strides in the last fifteen years that I sometimes wonder if my children still know what a boiler is.[3]

3. An enormous metal container which weighed a ton when it had to be heaved up on to the gas stove full of water, soap powder and dirty nappies. Absolute murder! I still used one for my older children, and never cease marvelling at the fact that each time I change one of my little grandchildren I throw everything into a perfumed plastic bag!

Not all young parents, however, take advantage of the new methods available to them. They tend to try and make their children relive the habits and behaviour of their own childhood which they look back at through rose-coloured spectacles. They think that in doing this they are handing something on to their children, but they're running the risk of complicating their lives unnecessarily by denying themselves the opportunity of improving their quality of life.

The sponge cake may come out of a Mr Kipling packet, or the steak and kidney pudding may have been replaced by a toasted cheese sandwich, but what does it matter as long as it's given to you in a cosy atmosphere by a mummy or daddy you love. I've been able to understand this ever since a young American woman living in Paris admitted to me that her idea of bliss was to take herself off to a genuine McDonalds at lunch time on a Sunday and buy herself a hamburger and a large Coke full of ice cubes, served in a cardboard tumbler. Tastes that remind people of their pasts are really very personal.

Resorting to out-of-date methods which consume vast amounts of time and energy certainly shouldn't put a stop to the 'family business', as long as you acknowledge the fact that you are employing them for your own pleasure and don't expect any other reward than the indulgent, egotistical satisfaction you get out of them.

If a mother likes spending ten minutes every morning plaiting her daughter's hair, let her do so. If she curses every day because the morning hairdo means she may miss her train, she would do much better to have her little girl's hair cut short. Her daughter certainly wasn't the one who wanted her hair in plaits just like her mother's when she was a little girl!

I can't recommend highly enough to those going into the 'family business' that they should search for every possible way of simplifying their lives because the opportunities of complicating them will be the ones they miss least.

6. Plan indestructible surroundings

One day, when I was discussing the reasons for Germany's falling birthrate with a German friend, she maintained that her compatriots' low fertility was to a large extent due to their hyper-cleanliness.

> 'In the old days, you could have a spotless house and several children at the same time, because housewives cleaned and tidied their houses the whole time. Also, respect for their surroundings was more important than comfort for the inhabitants. You had to wear slippers so as not to dirty the parquet floor, the children took off their wet clothes as soon as they came in, and no-one put their feet on the armchairs or put glasses down on the polished furniture.
>
> Nowadays it's impossible to enforce this sort of discipline. The moment you have two children in a small flat, it's a shambles – the sort of chaos that faces working mothers when they come home in the evenings, which they have neither the courage nor the time to tidy up every day. German women, having had to choose between their house and children, have chosen their house.'

I began protesting, and accusing her of running down her fellow countrywomen: such materialism sounded to me like something in a cartoon, it was so unbelievable. Then we thought a bit harder, and it came to us that other European countries with the reputation of having the cleanest houses – Switzerland, Sweden and Holland, have equally low birthrates. In the case of Switzerland, it is the only possible explanation for such a low birthrate in a country that has neither had an economic crisis nor an unemployment rate approaching that of its neighbours! In a recent *Newsweek* enquiry into couples who have decided not to have children, a young family counsellor from Los Angeles described how much she appreciates her sophisticated surroundings when she comes home in the evenings. Her house is full of stumbling blocks for children, which totally preclude their presence. Her divan is covered in ivory-coloured silk, and her black lacquered floors need to be continually wiped with a duster to get rid of people's footmarks.

'One day my husband and I had a good laugh thinking that if we had children there would be nowhere for them to go except the porch!'[4]

If the fashion for immaculate interiors with bedspreads made of exorbitant materials and lacquered floors really means banning children from our households, then give me washable paint, loose covers and white wood furniture! Whatever the French poet Lamartine may say, inanimate objects don't have souls, neither can they give you loving looks or feelings. They are there to help you enjoy life – provided there is some!

Once the children have left you'll have plenty of time to match your chair covers to your white hair and your curtains to your silk dressing gowns.

7. Make children fit into your lives

There is the ideal and there is reality.

The ideal would be: to put the children to bed at eight o'clock every evening, to serve up meals at regular hours, to give them green vegetables instead of chips and spaghetti bolognaise, not to let them go out when they have a slight cold and to take them somewhere healthy for their holidays even if it means Mummy can't swim and sunbathe, etc.

Reality is: if both parents work, the children go to bed too late; eating dinner without rushing and enjoying a bit of time with them afterwards means that the children are often allowed to go to sleep in front of the television even if they have to be carried to bed; you give them spaghetti rather than have a fight about whether they eat their greens; you take them on holiday to Spain where they get horribly sunburnt, and keep Spanish hours, etc.

4. *Newsweek*, 1 September 1986.

The era of perfect parents is no more. The American supermum, who is a willing slave to her children, can't manage two things at once – she can't be both a career woman and an English nanny. Today's parents try to do the maximum, but they can't do the impossible.

Last winter I went to dinner with a friend who has three children herself. She had invited two other couples: one of them had arrived with a four-year old and a tiny baby in a carrycot, and the other with a six-year old. The mildest description of the evening was 'disturbed' until the three Indians stopped doing a war dance round the table and fell fast asleep in a heap on the carpet. (I must point out that it was a Saturday evening, so they were able to recover from their exertions the next morning.)

You couldn't possibly have imagined such a scene when I was young. You either went out without your children, or you stayed at home and put them to bed at eight and made sure they went to sleep. However, I think that parents are right to go out – it's better to let the children fit in with the parents' lives than to make them feel frustrated because they are having to fit in with their children's lives.

A lot of paediatricians would certainly disagree with this principle. But aren't they the first to admit that having fun is one of the best tonics?

8. Learn to delegate

This is more or less superfluous advice, since 'needs must'. Most women work, so they have to hand over their children, particularly the young ones, to someone during the day. In France, grandmothers are top of the list (67.5% of working mothers are helped by their family), next come child minders who are mainly 'moonlighters', and day nurseries are way down the list with only 10% of the children to look after. Two-thirds of under-school age children are looked after outside, while a third are lucky enough to be looked after in their own homes.

These figures prove that the parent/minder relationship is on a highly personal level. Therefore it is vital that delegating is done in a confident and relaxed way. This has often been pointed out with the children's well-being in mind. I'm recommending it here for the parents' peace of mind, particularly the mother's. It's impossible to work properly all day long if you are worrying all the time about what's going on with the children and whoever is meant to be looking after them.

Young entrepreneurs know that they can no longer be absolute masters over their affairs, but only leaders of the orchestra. They are liable to get into difficulties if they can't leave others to carry out certain duties which they have delegated. Young parents have to do the same if they're not going to go through hell, worrying every day.

An accountant called Veronica had no confidence in her little girl's minder. Her career was in danger because the thought of finding a sad-eyed, neglected little girl each evening made her unable to concentrate on her columns of figures. Having changed minders four times, she ended up working part-time, three days a week. The little girl stayed with her grandmother on those three days. Veronica returned to her senses and got her sums right.

Please don't think I'm saying grannie is the only solution. Sometimes she's worse than other people when it comes to delegating, especially if she's a maternal grandmother – which is nearly always the case – and the young mother totally disagrees with her own mother's methods of upbringing without daring to say so, or being able to argue about them as she could with a paid minder. At other times it's the father who jibs at the granny's presence without daring to say so.

It doesn't really matter who you have confidence in. The important thing is to find that particular person. From that moment, everything in the garden is lovely, for the parents as well as the children!

9. Have a clear conscience

In order to be parents, and not victims, this is without doubt the most essential requirement – an extremely revolutionary attitude, given current thinking! We've already seen (Chapter III) how everything in modern psychology and teaching methods has joined forces in order to accuse parents. Everything is their fault, and they are responsible for everything – everything that goes wrong, naturally.

Which brings me back once again to my half-full cup. Apart from a few who have serious health or personality problems, nearly all today's children are great fun. They're more independent, more lively, more resourceful and more forward than their cosseted predecessors whose mothers were over protective.

These days, young working mothers seem to be more relaxed than those of the preceding generation, and it looks as though they may turn out to be the dominant type. In the last few years, they have become the majority, and wives who stay at home will be in the minority from now on. Curiously enough, there has been a subtle change in public opinion – as a working mother you are no longer considered 'bad', as opposed to 'good' if you stay at home.

One evening I popped in to see my daughter-in-law and give the children a hug. She had just come back from a hard day at the office, consisting of non-stop meetings. Her two sons leaped at her and hung round her neck (a seven-stone bear hug is just too heavy!) telling her both at once and at the tops of their voices about the marks they got that day, the exercise books they'd lost, the note to excuse the one with the cold from PE, the felt tip one had pinched from the other. . . . The din made you feel like shooting yourself. This was their mother's reaction:

> 'Boys, I've had an exhausting day, and I need to rest for half an hour. Be nice and go to your room – you can play or listen to a tape – or fight if you feel like it. I'll call you when I feel better, and then we can have a nice chat about everything.'

She took off her shoes, put her feet up, and the boys went off. Half an hour later, when they were allowed out, they really didn't seem to have a grudge against anyone!

I was really impressed by my daughter-in-law's attitude because I would have been quite incapable of doing the same thing at her age. Riddled with guilt, like all other career women of my generation, I had a conscience about my children the whole time. I never left them from the moment I came home until their bedtime, with the result that I often snapped at them because they wore me out, and I was in no fit state to put up with their whingeing and gesticulating. I thought my daughter-in-law's method was much more effective, and beneficial all round. To put up with children you need to be in the right state of mind in the first place. A guilty conscience is a very bad guide when it comes to bringing up children. It's easier said than done, I know, but it really is better to leave your conscience hanging up in the cloakroom when you come home after a day's work. Fathers get away from the 'perfect parents' myth more readily than mothers – they know how to live *with* children, not only *for* children.

10. Have confidence in the future

'I promise the child born today that his life will be twice as easy as his parents'.'
        Charles de Gaulle, President of the Republic
        14 June 1960, 21 hours, televised speech.

I know this sentence by heart, it's even engraved on a christening mug. I was having my third son while de Gaulle was pronouncing it. That's why we've never forgotten this incredibly inaccurate forecast in our family.

The crisis put a stop to the expected economic expansion of the consumer society. The babies born in June 1960, who are now mainly of working age, are facing the problem of unemployment in all the Western countries. Materially speaking, their lives will by no means be twice as easy as their parents'.

Will their lives be twice as happy? That's another story, General. Happiness isn't only a question of cash. Some children's lives probably will be more difficult; they may not find it easy to fit into a society which doesn't have jobs for everyone – they will have more emotional break-ups, and will find themselves left on their own more frequently. Others, on the other hand, will find ways of fulfiling themselves that just didn't exist twenty years ago – they will lead richer, more creative lives than their parents, and will form rewarding and loving relationships with one or more partners. Who knows?

Certainly not presidents or professional soothsayers. And parents even less!

How do you know, when you give life to someone, what sort of a life that's going to be?

It's my opinion that if you want to go into the 'family business' you shouldn't think further than your heart tells you to. All you can do is to give your children the opportunity of making a life for themselves – you can't guarantee what sort of life that will be. Never before has a constantly changing society made the future of a new-born child so unpredictable. Children won't take after us, or very few of them will, they aren't born to be like us, they're born to be themselves.

If we can't guarantee them a future, let's at least give them a present!

Is having children a risky undertaking? Yes, absol-utely, no-one would deny that. Dear Mr Peguy, you're right, parents really are the modern-day adventurers, except for one small difference. You only talked about fathers and, believe me, today the adventure is much more risky and complicated for mothers who have to be every-thing at once.

However, there isn't any reason why these entre-preneur-parents should take sole financial and moral responsibility for what is a vital part of national life. The powers-that-be, having a healthy respect for private enter-prise, take steps to encourage the setting up of businesses; they help them to get going, and give them incentives to take on employees and to invest. There should be a similar effort to encourage the creation of children, to help them get going, and to give incentives to widen the family circle.

The time has really come for those in charge to tackle these problems at the highest possible level. It's a question of survival!

X

Proposals To The Authorities

In a Western democracy there's no such thing as a standard list of precise measures which would be enough to increase the birthrate from one day to the next – or rather, in just over nine months! We can only be sure of one thing: extra allowances for families 'do something'.

Each country has its own traditions, public opinion, historical precedents, financial limits and electoral considerations. To talk about French policy towards the birthrate in Germany would be quite irrelevant – Spaniards may not be as concerned about the pros and cons of the birthrate as Canadians, and the British exchequer doesn't have the same resources as the Swiss Ministry of Finance. However, everywhere you go, people's lifestyles are getting closer, and they are becoming more similar in outlook and behaviour. People are working out a new pattern for their existence, and it's still possible that children will form an integral part of it, provided the collective will is in favour of them. It's said that the general interest isn't the sum total of people's private interests: neither is the collective will the sum total of people's private wishes. The proof of this is that millions of young adults currently have vague desires for children which don't get fulfilled. They're not living in the sort of environment to push them in the right direction and give them general encouragement – what they need is a sort of social rehabilitation. The creation of such an 'infantiphile' atmosphere should be the responsibility of all sectors of government.

All you in power, whether you're in politics, economics, social services, medicine or culture, and whether your responsibility is national, local or municipal, over to you! It's obvious what's at stake: you can either create a positive climate with all sorts of support for young parents to enable them to carry out their desire for children, or one-child families – if you can really call them families – will remain in the ascendancy.

As I'm addressing my remarks to those of you in power, there's no need for me to stress the importance of this challenge for the future of the nation, which you serve or represent. Which of you MPs could be short-sighted enough nowadays not to view the falling birthrate as a dangerous sign of decline? A country where people don't want to bring up children is sick, however high its standard of living, or however democratic it may be. In this respect, the United States is currently going through a more serious crisis than its President seems to realize. The number of childless couples has doubled in twenty years, and is still on the increase. One married woman in four between the age of twenty-five and thirty-four is now childless. This isn't too serious yet because the present generation of thirty-year olds, who are the result of the baby boom, is very numerous, but what's going to become of the American family in the year 2000?

You in authority, whether you have a lot of influence, or not very much, you can't neglect the positive element represented by a nation's young parents, especially those who are daring and adventurous enough to have a 'real' family with several children. You can't get out of your responsibility to them. Whether they sail through life with an ample, well-disciplined crew, or have to haul in their sails and reduce the crew to an absolute minimum will depend on your attitudes, your encouragement and your achievements. In the worse cases, the very concept of the family might disappear, and all you'll have left will be small, individual units with no-one to revolve round them.

I'm not going to give a detailed list here of all the laws and payments which would have to be changed or allocated to achieve a 'family policy' or a 'birthrate policy'. I don't

like these two expressions – the first one conveys a terribly
moralizing and out-of-date impression as it makes the
'family' out to be very upright and good, and casts a critical
and scornful eye over the happy but wicked lovers with
their only child. The second one is even more ghastly, some
kind of state-controlled ogre which exploits children for its
prestige or its economic needs. I'm not very keen on East
Germany's baby-athletes, even though their rich crop of
medals makes them the object of admiration by the
sporting public everywhere!

Let's come back to our 'infantiphile atmosphere'.
Here are a few suggestions I'd like to make to the
authorities to help them get into this new state of mind:

1. Worry about the important, not only the urgent

Yes, I know, people in Western countries have plenty of
other hobby-horses to flog – there are economic crises,
unemployment, terrorism, drugs, AIDS, delinquency and
upheavals and disasters of every kind. All today's hobby-
horses are sad ones, their nostrils distended with fear, but
the one I'm trying to interest you in is happy, positive,
enterprising and optimistic, and you will want to stroke it
because of its bright future and its promise to try and
change a stressful today and a jaded tomorrow.

In senior management courses, one of the first things
they teach you is to distinguish between urgent and
important. Then they follow this up by telling managers
they mustn't allow themselves to get swamped by a myriad
urgent, everyday tasks, but must devote the major part of
their time and energy to important decisions which will
affect the future.

The birthrate is just the sort of important problem that
people have been pushing to one side for years in order to
deal with urgent problems. Nevertheless, if you broach the
subject with a politician, no matter what side he's on, he
will admit that youth is a nation's trump card, and that an
ageing nation represents a latent danger. Very few people

are prepared to go further, and pass on the benefits they got out of life to others not yet born.

Maybe what we need are one or two influential people to carry the torch for this cause. After all, babies with no other word attached must be just as valuable as baby-seals or baby-trees! There's not much point in worrying about the environment if there are no humans left in it!

2. Be daring – don't be afraid of shocking people!

If you want to carry people along with you, you mustn't be afraid of facing up to reality and saying so. I long to find a man or woman in the public eye with the courage to be provocative and defend certain principles. For instance:

– Children are a benefit for the entire nation, and therefore it's not fair that we parents should be almost exclusively responsible for them when, as working people and contributors, we have to support the unemployed, the sick – those who are really ill, but also the hypochondriacs whose medicine cupboards are bursting with pills they don't take – alcoholics, crazy drivers, medal-hunting sportsmen (not always), old people, coalminers made redundant at fifty, long-term prisoners, not to mention our armed forces. . . .

Children are the poor relations when it comes to distributing manna from heaven to the public!

– Workers shouldn't all get the same allowances; their family status should be taken into account, and preference should be given to parents in general and mothers in particular. At first sight, the recent French law bringing in a uniform, thirty-nine hour week instead of a forty-hour one seemed a fair decision but in fact it's completely arbitrary. Where's the justice in giving a childless single woman the same hours as a mother who has to fit twice as much into her day with housework to do as well as a job. It would be much better to let the single woman work forty hours and grant the mother a thirty-five-hour week.

Mothers with young children should be given priority

when it comes to part-time jobs, and guarantees of re-employment after the birth of a baby should be extended. In addition to equality between men and women, which isn't always respected, there should be a system of preference for mothers and fathers.

– Children are everybody's business. There's no reason why the birthrate should cost business sectors such as service industries who employ mainly women, more than others. Why not institute a National Birthrate Fund to see to the sharing out of costs between various businesses? The burden of absences on maternity leave would be more evenly divided, and employers would be less reluctant to take on women of child bearing age.

– Indirect taxation is more of a burden on household budgets than direct taxation. Whenever there is talk of tax reductions, it's always in income tax. Wouldn't it be possible to remove VAT, or anyway reduce it, on a whole series of consumer goods which are essential for parents who have a second or third child? Take cars for instance: on presentation of a full Family Allowance book a purchaser could be given tax relief on a bigger car. Airline passengers get huge tax reductions on perfume, alcohol and tobacco, so why not do the same sort of thing for fathers who need bigger cars for their growing families?

Quite apart from the economic angle, such a measure could have a symbolic value.

a) It would demonstrate up-to-date thinking, by acknowledging the important part played by the car in a family's budget and way of life. Reductions in rail fares still exist for large families even though three-quarters of all households own a car, and the more children you have, the less you travel by train. You wouldn't dream of travelling by *train* with three children if you were going on holiday or out to Sunday lunch with Granny and Grandpa!

b) For once, it would be aimed at fathers, doing them a good turn which would undoubtedly benefit everyone including wives and children, but would perhaps mean more to a man.

c) It would mark the recognition of parents who over the

years have produced and developed a commodity vital to the national good, in other words its children.

3. Be up-to-date: don't hark back to the old ways

In twenty years most women have changed places, from the hearth to the workplace; couples have changed and have given up their predominant role, and children have changed their living conditions. At the same time, most European countries and the United States persist in thinking along old-fashioned lines.

Because life is economically, psychologically and socially different with two salaries than it was with one, this movement continues to get stronger. It had been thought that unemployment would put a stop to the ever-increasing number of women in employment, but this has been far from the case. Mothers are increasingly reluctant to give up their jobs in order to bring up their children. If they do agree to stop work for one, two or three years, or to work half-or part-time so they can look after their children when they're tiny, they're still quite determined to get another job as soon as their children are a little older. If you question women, you soon realize that this movement isn't going to come to an end. We're not going to go back to the families of yesterday, with Daddy as the breadwinner and Mummy as the full-time pan-scrubber. In the United States, only one household in ten consists of 'old time' families like this. As long as the term 'mother' continues to be confused with 'mother at home', we shall discourage rather than encourage young people from having children.

The alternative 'two salaries or three children'? which I've come across several times while doing research for this book, shouldn't be put to people in this way, because it produces a virtually automatic reply, i.e. that couples would rather keep two salaries. To hell with a third child if it means the wife giving up her job indefinitely!

On the other hand, supposing more flexible, modern and progressive solutions were put forward:

- A full-time salary, or a part-time salary and three children?

- Two part-time jobs for a few years and three children?

- One sole salary for three years, to be topped up by a maternity allowance followed by a guaranteed return to work and second salary for whichever partner stayed at home to look after the baby, and three children?

I'm not saying that all mothers with only children would immediately go ahead and have a second child, given these sort of alternatives, or that all parents with two children would start a third, but couples who have a nagging desire for lots of babies would probably be more inclined to give in to it.

4. Don't be afraid of diversity: forget fixed ideas

It's becoming quite usual for the under-forties to do things in a variety of ways. As we've seen, personal situations can be very different, and people can no longer be cast in any particular mould – some people co-habit, some are married, divorced, remarried, divorced and living together again without bothering to remarry, and some think of themselves as couples without actually living together, etc. This doesn't bother anyone any more, apart from a few disconcerted grandparents, who will keep on asking the young couples during family lunches:

'So when's this wedding going to be?'

'Soon, Granny, very soon . . .'

Much more significant is the fact that in a person's lifetime there are many different, successive phases. Ardent lovers decide to get married in order to have a party or a child. Husbands and wives, who were married before God 'till death us do part', get divorced. Lovers resolutely refuse to go to the altar although to all intents and purposes they've been living together for years in wedded bliss. Families expand or shrink according to the way couples get together, separate or are kept in touch by their children.

Children's relationships to one another get very complicated when they're no longer only related by blood, but also by the ebb and flow of their parents' emotions, thus forming groups of children who are legitimate, natural, 'steps', 'in-laws', 'out-laws', 'ex-es', temporary and future.

As the young say, 'You'll just have to put up with it . . .'

It's vital not to disapprove of this profusion by harking back to the traditional family where everyone has the same name. You might well arouse antagonism just when people seem to be better disposed towards marriage. Young people want to find out for themselves what suits them – they want to decide their own way of thinking, their own lifestyles, their own image. Your job is to be adaptable to their way of doing things and to be fair to everyone, not to lay down the law to them about how they should run their lives.

Let's take the example of marriage in French law. As the result of an incredible anachronism in tax regulations, which is currently under revision, married couples who were both working were actually treated less fairly than unmarried couples, especially when the man and woman earned approximately the same amount. This situation was clearly unfair and illogical, because it meant that married couples were penalized and a lot of unmarried couples were put off getting married.

In practice, taxation shouldn't have any bearing on whether you decide to get married or not because its not up to society to interfere directly or indirectly in what is after all a purely personal decision. Future couples should be able to opt for the tax system most suitable to them, in just the same way as they can choose the sort of marriage settlement they like. It's fine to review the legislation in order to stop it penalizing married couples, but it mustn't be a question of favouring the 'legal' at the expense of the 'illegal'.

I don't understand why some people are absolutely obsessed with the idea that the number of marriages must at all costs correspond with the birthrate. They were certainly dependent on one another in the past, but it seems to me that the connection is much less clear-cut these days, when some people have babies *without* being married, others get married *in order* to have a baby, others get married *because* they've had a baby and others still don't have babies *even though* they're married.

Personally, I think it's a pity that young people don't appreciate the rich symbolism of a public commitment when they decide to make a go of living together. An 'official' marriage is a way of announcing your union to the rest of the world, and is well worth experiencing at least once in a life-time. This ancient ceremony has been part of human existence since the dawn of time. Like all traditional ritual, it's full of meaning, and very emotional. Yet it's still an individual matter – religious for some people, purely convenient for others, and politics should keep its nose right out of it.

5. Don't confuse the birthrate with social justice

It's quite simple: each time a government plans to give priority to families, it's held back by its fear of penalizing other social categories. A nation's resources being neither infinite nor inexhaustible you can only give to one section at a time – you can't give to everyone. Because these days there are many more men and women in Western democracies with few or no children than there are with two or more, any measure to increase the birthrate is likely to annoy more electors than it satisfies, particularly if any 'rich'[1] are included amongst parents with three children or more for whose benefit these measures would be intended.

To hell with all the 'sour grapes' merchants! Whatever they may say, the 'rich' should, by all possible means, be

1. Just as there is really no longer a simple division of 'left' and 'right', but rather one of 'social democrats/liberal/conservative', you can't talk about 'rich' and 'poor' any more in Western democracies, but rather about 'disadvantaged/subsidized' and 'free–spending independents'. The real 'rich' only represent a tiny minority.

encouraged to have lots of chidren. Firstly, because they're more likely to give in to the temptation of having a large family, which would be less of a drain on their resources than it would on less privileged people, secondly, because any children they may have will cost much less to the nation and lastly because 'poor little rich children' are super-consumers – they keep industry and commerce going if you think of toys, clothes, electronics, corner shops, pleasure grounds, etc. . . .

If your 'left-wing' conscience is shocked by all this sort of thing, just console yourself by remembering that children constitute the best possible way there is of impoverishing parents – surely it's better to impoverish the rich than the poor!

6. Try to give time off rather than money

'Time is money', as the Anglo-Saxons say. I agree, but the opposite isn't always the case. Having money doesn't necessarily give you time, especially where children are concerned.

First, working hours: most mothers ask for more flexibility in their hours even if it means giving up some of their salary. Economic considerations rather than the government decide how people organize their time off. If the stranglehold working hours have on people could be loosened, wage earners would be able to both keep their jobs and bring up all the children they want. In a lot of businesses it would not only be possible, but it might also be desirable to introduce flexitime, and suit everyone's hours to their needs. Do people still need to be reminded that a workforce that is less pressurized by strict working hours and has a more relaxed timetable would produce higher quality goods and better service?

Time needs to be rationalized in everyday life just as much as in professional life. Mothers who stay at home also need to relax and have time to themselves. Anything that could be done to give them a few hours away from their little darlings would be in the public interest.

When shopping one Sunday morning at *Ikea*, I had to admire the initiative of this Swedish chain of shops which sell 'Everything for the house'. They've installed a nursery on the ground floor of each branch where young couples can leave their little children of two to six while they get on with their shopping. I'm sure it's commercially profitable – demographically, it's brilliant! Just imagine being able to leave your tiny children at every supermarket entrance and doing the weekly shop in peace. What a treat for parents! Town councils should go even further than this, and increase the number of day nurseries. Even if you had to pay, such nurseries would give to a much wider spectrum the chance of getting away from their children for a few hours, something that has become a rare luxury for parents these days.

Baby-sitters should be re-organized in various districts, and more of them should be made official – parents should be able to get themselves out of a fix by simply picking up the receiver. There are bound to be occasional 'panic stations' when you have little children at home, and no-one really seems to have given this a thought.

Some town councils in France have taken on unemployed youngsters to pick up litter in public gardens, but I've never heard of them being asked to look after children in these gardens to help their desperately over-burdened mothers, who are voters after all. All the same, children could provide a never-ending supply of 'odd jobs'. For that matter, 'nannies' should be encouraged to stage a comeback – the 'below stairs' side of their job should be removed, and the educative aspect brought out more.

The system of 'au pair' girls who look after children for a few hours a week without ever being considered 'domestics' works perfectly well for foreigners, so why not organize a similar one on a large scale for girls from one's own country? Do you really need to be Swedish in order to look after English children, or English in order to look after French children? Don't let anyone give me the argument about children learning a foreign language. It's almost always the 'au pair' girls who learn, hardly ever the children!

7. Reassure young mothers by giving them long-term guarantees

It's no good pretending – the threat of divorce does hang over the birthrate. A lot of young women hesitate to become mothers because they're afraid they will find themselves living on their own, divorced or separated, without adequate provision for the children's upbringing.

They are right to be afraid. A recent survey showed that one-third of alimonies is never paid, and the remaining two-thirds are paid spasmodically. This is a really shocking situation because it deprives children of any guaranteed funds.

Imagine what would happen if we stopped paying old people their pensions which they rely on for their survival: the scandal would rock society from top to bottom. The fact that children are deprived of funds because their fathers refuse to help support them doesn't seem to arouse public opinion to any great extent – it's not a subject of discussion in the media. Nevertheless, grim stories of defaulting ex-husbands are rife in all female circles. They've haunted young women for years, and scare them more than ever – there's no real sign of improvement, even though the law has become more and more strict. The authorities can't be complacent and claim that they have got a policy under way to improve the birthrate until they take the bull by the horns and tackle this problem properly.

The other long-term problem is pensions. According to our system, pensions are almost always based on salaries and working conditions. The longer you work and the more you earn, the better off you will be when you retire. This system takes virtually no account of your family circumstances.

Take my own example – it's always the one you know best!

A woman of my age, who has had the same career with approximately the same salary for the same number of years will get exactly the same pension as I will, whether she's had any children or not. In my opinion this system is absolutely iniquitous because, although the woman referred to may have paid a bit more in income tax, she's sure to have saved more of her salary than I could. This way of calculating pensions on a strictly financial basis is ludicrous: the less children you have, the better off you are in retirement – a retirement which has to a large extent been guaranteed and paid for by other people's children. Personally, I think that the contributions paid by our children, once they have become working adults, should benefit us, their parents, in preference to childless elderly people. (When I'm old, I really will feel secure with four sons working!)

Marc Ullmann, a French radio commentator, who is also in favour of this link between parents and children, writes:

> 'It is vital to try and find a way of reviving a tradition as old as the hills, by which old people's comfort depended on the affluence and number of their children. All that needs to be done is to establish a link between working children's increased contributions and their parents' increased pensions . . . Those who would benefit most from such a system would be old people who had not only had lots of children, but had also given them the sort of education to guarantee they did well in life and were eligible to pay large amounts in contributions. . . .
>
> Therefore, we must somehow or other turn the tide so that babies become "investments", and constitute a guarantee for their parents' future wellbeing.'

Children already are a good emotional 'investment'. If in the long run they proved financially 'profitable' as well, how would anyone be able to resist having several of them, in order to guarantee themselves a comfortable old age?

After all, it's a much more pleasant prospect than taking out a life insurance.

8. Give children a better image, especially in men's eyes

With a bit of cash, some clear ideas and a good advertising agency, you can get people to do things they wouldn't have dreamt of doing a few years earlier. Would you like few examples of near-miracles accomplished by the media? Smoking has been considerably reduced in the States, drinking has been somewhat reduced in France, middle-aged people have taken up sport. . . .

No-one's going to convince me that, with a few delightful pictures and some touching, persuasive arguments slotted into prime viewing time, it wouldn't be just as easy to arouse the desire for children that's lying waiting to be rekindled in so many young people.

However, if you want to revive the paternal streak, it's no good showing only the domestic aspect of devoted fatherhood. Men aren't going to be bowled over by burnt, mushed-up vegetables or dirty nappies. They'd much rather daydream about older children who ask them questions, who like doing the things they like doing, and gaze at them admiringly because Daddy is the strongest, the cleverest, . . . the greatest. Children are the only ones who are completely sincere when they look at you like that. Men covet these sorts of looks – they need them even, now that women no longer find men 'more' everything than they are themselves! If you want women to be mothers, all you need to do is to show them babies. For men, a better bet is to show them the next size up – three-year-olds and upwards. Daddy can *already* talk to them, and they're *still* interested in what Daddy has to say. A few mini cover-girls and boys, used to good effect in television ads, would certainly do a lot more for the birthrate than discussions between dry old economists.

9. Show singleness of purpose and stick to your guns

Governments come and go, but children are always there –
in fact, they're the only things you can't get rid of even
when you can no longer afford to look after them. The
house, the car or the telephone can respectively be sold,
given back or cut off, but not children! The time has passed
when they could be abandoned in church porches. Once
parents have had a baby, they're 'lumbered' with him for
twenty years. At least!

A country should be as consistent as its parents. It
should honour its commitments during the whole of a
child's upbringing, and shouldn't allow its 'family' policies
to fluctuate according to the whims of succeeding prime
minsters or chancellors of the exchequer. It's monstrous
that parents should suddenly be expected to give up the
privileges they had been promised when they decided to
have more children. It should be possible to sign a valid
'upbringing contract' guaranteeing that the clauses which
were in force when the child was born should be respected
until he attains his majority.

Such permanence would obviously mean that there
would have to be agreement between those of different
political persuasions so that the first act of a new government wouldn't consist of systematically doing the opposite
of its predecessor.

I can't help feeling that agreement over a matter such
as the birthrate should be possible. When a country's future
is endangered, it always manages to get a 'consensus'. The
birthrate is one of those dangers which will come to a head
in the future – and it requires singleness of purpose and
sticking to one's guns. Just like military strategy, it entails a
relentless pursuit of the same objectives if it's to have any
chance of succeeding.

Such collaboration already exists to try and prevent
death. Couldn't we institute it to encourage life?

All this should take place fairly quickly – we must take
advantage of the present generation's new thinking, with its
renewed respect for family values. The desire for children

doesn't just come about on its own, it needs to be cultivated. Small seeds are being blown about by this wind of change, but they can only take root in fertile ground – unless they find some, they will be scattered by a wind of indifference.

Conclusion

To The Daughter I Never Had

Mary, you would have been twenty-five by now. I'm sure of your age because you had been expected (once again. . . !) between your two younger brothers. But your future was cut short while you were still in the womb – I was fated never to have a daughter!

I've often missed you since. I would have loved the challenge of bringing up a girl in this modern world (if only to get away from the toy cars and footballs which cluttered up my existence as a mother of four boys). Although bringing you up would have been easier than it would have been in the past – I'd like to think that we'd have been able to discuss every aspect of your life frankly and openly – it would also have been more complicated than bringing up boys. How would I have explained to you how to consider yourself as good as a man without losing your femininity? All my friends who have daughters, and can see the conflicts that today's young women have to face up to, tell me how lucky I am to have only boys. I don't agree with them.

Because, you see, I adore being a woman; I've never wanted to be a man. I've always thought how lucky I was to be able to live through the second half of the 20th century as a woman.

Not only are we able to conduct our lives 'like boys', but we have kept the privilege of bearing children as well![1]

1. I deliberately said 'privilege', not 'handicap'. I've got no wish for men to be 'pregnant' – I would rather we remained the only ones able to carry out that function! Anyway, do you really think they'd argue with us over this?

That's why I worry so much when I see all these young women agonizing and humming and hawing at the idea of having children. They're afraid they would be a drag on their lives. But, Mary, *life above all means* children! All the rest is certainly important, but only relatively so. You mustn't 'choose' between children and the rest of life, you must want everything all together. It'll certainly take a few generations to think up ways of organizing this new system for living. You would have led the way, Mary, and your daughter would have taken over from you.

I couldn't help thinking about you a lot while writing this book. Often, one can be very broad-minded in theory, but the only way of putting one's convictions to the test is by finding out what your own personal reactions would be in certain circumstances. (It's all very well to say you're anti-racist, but it's not so easy to welcome your child's mixed marriage with open arms!) Therefore, now that you would have been the right age to fall in love and get married, I've often wondered what my attitude would have been towards you as a potential mother. Would I have advised you to wait a bit and enjoy life before having babies? Would I have encouraged you to be a young mother because, once the first few years are over, you can really enjoy your children as friends? Would I have been happy to know you were expecting a baby? Would I have worried that you'd get too exhausted coping with children and a career?

First of all, knowing you were pregnant, I'd have felt very emotional. I know I'd have shed a few tears when you told me you were expecting a baby. Being incurably sentimental, I'm already reaching for the packet of Kleenex the moment the heroine whispers a few inaudible words into the ear of the man she loves (you can tell by his expression that she's murmuring to him about a 'happy event'!). I have damp eyes every time they show that fantastic moment on the television when a crumpled, new-born baby is laid in his mother's arms. It's a moment I'll never forget, when you feel as if your heart is going to burst. I can share it intensely with women I don't even know.

Being consistent myself, Mary, I would certainly

advise you to give your first baby a brother or sister very soon to keep him company, and relieve your guilt at not being able to spend enough time with him. I would worry a little, knowing your life would be complicated and tiring for a few years – nevertheless, I would comfort myself by remembering that I survived that period – and even enjoyed life – in spite of an existence that was overflowing with children and work. Maybe over the years you can forget the irritations of everyday life, and just remember how much love it brought you?

As to whether you have a third child, well, it's much too early to think of that yet. The joy you get from the first two will encourage you to have more such little sources of happiness.

So far, it's all plain sailing, and I stand by everything I've written in this book. I only hope that your life as a mother will be as 'uneventful' as mine, a routine sort of life with its judicious mixture of problems, joys, hard work, pleasures, battles, reconciliations, disappointments and achievements!

* * *

That's all too simple. My prognostications sound like something out of a romantic magazine:

'Mary is twenty-five, and lives with the man she loves. They are very happy and decide to have some children. Mary's mother is absolutely over the moon; she cries with joy when she learns she's going to be a grandmother . . .'

Life isn't always like that unfortunately!

In the first place, like more and more girls of your generation, you could decide not to have any children at all – it might not even enter your head, or you might postpone this aspect of your feminine nature until much later. In this case, what could I say to you? Nothing – obviously I would be very careful not to be insistent because it would soon change our relationship. If you don't want a child, no earthly pleading by your mother will make any difference. Your husband's the only person who might be able to convince you – and he would have to want a baby more than you do, which isn't very likely! My only hope is that reading this book might cause you both to reflect, and that your reflections might turn into desire.

My main hope is that you don't let your thousands of other interests keep you from being a mother. I know quite a lot of people – some of them couples, but mostly single women, who are reaching a childless old age. I don't know any of them who are really happy with such an unfettered existence, whose future holds no surprises for them. I really wouldn't like you to find yourself without children at my age, Mary.

When you're young, you hardly ever think of old age. How very long it must seem to those without families! I've done my sums and, with my large family, even if our relationships cool off a bit over the years and I only see each of my sons once a month, I would still see one child each week! I like the idea of not having to take up too much of each one's time. It's a good thing I didn't only have one child. Either I would have been very lonely, or he would have been driven mad!

Even if you don't find someone to share your life, Mary – and you're so pretty, it's hard to believe you won't – I would encourage you not to live without children. You can always adopt other people's children. My friend Frances did, and I can promise you that when she talks about her little kids her eyes shine and she purrs with maternal pride. I'm convinced you don't love children because you *create* them, but because *you share life* with them.

Finally, to go back to the question of a 'postponement' – you could find yourself going through a serious crisis – perhaps you could be expecting a baby by a man who refuses point-blank to have anything to do with it; or you're afraid of jeopardizing your studies or your career – or are about to get a divorce, etc. Then what would I advise you? You must see that I wouldn't dream of trying to influence you in cases like those. You're the only one who can decide whether to have a child or not. If it was going to cause insoluble problems in your life, and would be more than you could bear, then you must feel free to make your own decision. Besides, who says you're going to discuss it with me! But if deep down you still found you wanted to have a child, in spite of having every possible reason to get rid of it, I would stand by you and help you to bring it up. Wanting a child is the most precious thing in the world, and you should do everything you can to carry out such a wish. This conviction of mine is the result of a story I was told about twelve years ago. I'm going to tell it to you before I finally end this book.

On that day, one of my colleagues, another woman journalist, came into the editorial office where I was working. She closed the door, and I could tell she was about to confide in me. Her face was grey with fatigue, and I found it hard to believe what she told me because she had a little boy of two and was on the brink of divorce.

'Christiane, I'm pregnant. I haven't told anyone yet, but I've simply got to talk to someone about it. I'm having a baby.'

'You poor thing! What are you going to do? You can't keep it – surely you're not going to risk finding yourself divorced with two children? It's absolute madness! Thank goodness you can get an abortion!'

To cut a long story short, I was the arch-counsellor, laying down the law and refusing to take no for an answer. From the moment she started speaking it was quite obvious what she ought to do. I nearly shouted at her for being careless just when she was in such a terribly difficult situation! However, I did feel really sorry for her, and I would have done anything to help her. . . .

'No, I've given it a lot of thought, and I really want this child. I can't think why – it's probably the greatest mistake I've ever made in my life, but I want this baby more than anything in the world . . .'

As she said that, her expression seemed to radiate with some inner strength, endowing her with an inexplicable serenity in spite of the circumstances. I was at a loss to understand her feelings, but her deep conviction was beyond argument. She was determined to have this child, whatever happened. I hugged her to give her courage – she seemed to me both responsible and heroic. She was saying *yes* to this baby in exactly the same way as Antigone said *no* to Creon.

Six months later in the middle of her divorce, she gave birth to a gorgeous little girl.

She was one year old when my friend learned that her son was suffering from a dreadful disease known as myopathy, which is passed on by the mother, and can only be contracted by boys. When confronted with this awful disaster, she said to me:

'You know, all the time I was expecting my little girl I couldn't think why I wanted her so much. Ever since her brother became ill, I've thought about nothing else. I would never have dared to have another child in case I'd had a boy, but now I've got my daughter, for my son as well as for myself – she'll give us something to live for, and help us to overcome our suffering . . .'

Ever since then I've known for certain what made me want to write this book. . . .

Appendix 1

The principle fertility rates of Western countries in 1985 compared with those of a certain number of under-developed countries

West Germany	1.27
Belgium	1.49
Denmark	1.45
Spain (1983)	1.71
France	1.82
Italy	1.42
Netherlands	1.50
United Kingdom	1.78
Austria	1.46
Finland	1.65
Norway	1.68
Sweden	1.73
Switzerland	1.51
Algeria	7.00
Nigeria	7.10
India	4.50
Laos	6.00
Mexico	4.70
Honduras	6.50
Kenya	8.00
China	2.10

Appendix 2

Table 1: The 30 most populated countries in the world (estimated in 1985)

		Millions
1	China	1042
2	India	762
3	USSR	278
4	United States	239
5	Indonesia	168
6	Brazil	138
7	Japan	121
8	Bangladesh	101
9	Pakistan	99.2
10	Nigeria	91.2
11	Mexico	79.7
12	Federal Germany	61.0
13	Vietnam	60.5
14	Italy	57.4
15	Philippines	56.8
16	United Kingdom	56.4
17	France	55.0
18	Thailand	52.7
19	Turkey	52.1
20	Egypt	48.3
21	Iran	45.1
22	South Korea	42.7
23	Spain	38.5
24	Poland	37.3
25	Burma	36.9
26	Ethiopia	36.0
27	Zaire	33.1
28	South Africa	32.5
29	Argentina	30.6
30	Colombia	29.4
Total of above countries		3981.4
World total		4845

Table 2: Population projections for 2020

		Millions
1	China	1288
2	India	1246
3	USSR	364
4	United States	297
5	Indonesia	293
6	Nigeria	258
7	Brazil	251
8	Bangladesh	207
9	Pakistan	196
10	Mexico	151
11	Japan	127
12	Vietnam	102
13	Philippines	101
14	Turkey	97
15	Egypt	94
16	Zaire	93
17	Iran	91
18	Ethiopia	88
19	Thailand	85
20	Burma	72
21	Tanzania	71
22	South Africa	70
23	Kenya	68
24	South Korea	59
25	Morocco	59
26	France	57
27	United Kingdom	56
28	Italy	55
29	Algeria	53
30	Sudan	51
	Total of above countries	6100
	World total	**7760**

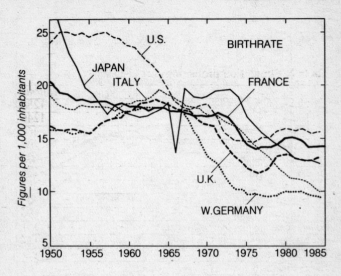

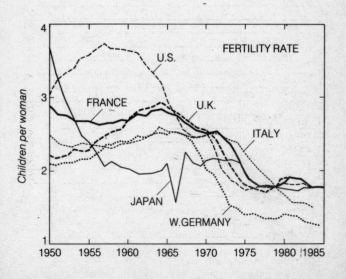

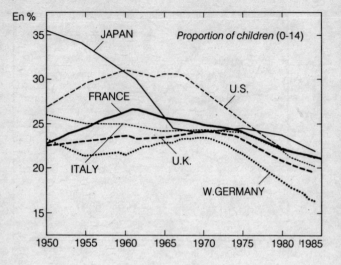